BE YOUR OWN
LITERARY AGENT

BE YOUR OWN
LITERARY AGENT

The Ultimate Insider's Guide
to Getting Published

Third Edition, Revised and Expanded

MARTIN P. LEVIN

Ten Speed Press
Berkeley / Toronto

A Kirsty Melville book

Ten Speed Press
Box 7123
Berkeley, California 94707
www.tenspeed.com

Distributed in Australia by Simon & Schuster Australia, in Canada by Ten Speed Press Canada, in New Zealand by Southern Publishers Group, in South Africa by Real Books, in Southeast Asia by Berkeley Books, and in the United Kingdom and Europe by Airlift Book Company.

The author and publisher would like to thank the following for permission to use previously published material: Gerald Gunther, author of *Learned Hand: The Man and the Judge* (Alfred A. Knopf, 1994); International Creative Management, Inc., *True Grit*, © 1969 by Charles Portis; from the book *Where Angels Walk: True Stories of Heavenly Visitors* by Joan Wester Anderson, © 1992 by Joan Wester Anderson, published by Barton & Brett Publishers, Inc.; Penguin Books, USA, Inc., from *Don Juan de Marco* by Jeremy Leven, novelization, Jean Blake White, © 1995 by New Line Productions, Inc. and Jeremy Leven, used by permission of Dutton Signet, a division of Penguin Books, USA, Inc.; Leading Publishers by Category on pp. 201–204 reprinted by permission of Open Book Publishing, Inc., Darien, CT, 203-316-8008.

Cover based on a design by Catherine Jacobes
Book design by Betsy Stromberg
Copyediting by Jean M. Blomquist

Library of Congress Cataloging-in-Publication Data

Levin, Martin P.
  Be your own literary agent : the ultimate insider's guide to getting published / Martin P. Levin.—3rd ed., rev. and expanded.
      p. cm.
"A Kirsty Melville book"—T.p. verso.
Includes bibliographical references and index.
  ISBN 1-58008-338-2
  1. Authorship—Marketing. 2. Literary agents. I. Title.
PN161 .L48 2002
070.5'2—dc21
                                   2001006278

Printed in Canada
First printing, this edition, 2002

1 2 3 4 5 6 7 8 9 10 — 06 05 04 03 02

Contents

The Tool Kit: Appendixes A–D

Preface to the Third Edition

Since the publication of the first edition of *Be Your Own Literary Agent* in 1995, I have heard from writers by mail, telephone, and e-mail. I have shared experiences with aspiring authors during and after my lectures throughout the country, and corresponded one-on-one with writers who reached me on America Online. I have also met with yet-to-be-published first-time authors each year at the Stanford Professional Publishing Course.

I am grateful to those who shared their experiences with me. Their experiences have helped me expand the book to make it even more useful. But most of all, my best source of reassurance has come from the hundreds of authors who have told me how this book has helped them get their books published without the assistance of an agent.

I would like to share portions of one piece of correspondence from author Hillary Davis, an American living in France:

> . . . thank you . . . for writing the book. I have had so much more luck, and much more quickly, not waiting for agents. And I have so enjoyed meeting publishers/editors, who were a joy to share ideas with. And now I have a draft agreement sitting in front of me on my desk waiting for me to sign, a dream for me. You gave me the added push to go try it on my own and saved me the heartache of waiting and nurturing an agent that STILL hasn't responded in a meaningful way.

This letter is typical of the many joyous stories readers have shared with me. I selected it from the hundreds of comments I have received because it emphasizes the point that authors can, with the information in this book, substitute action for anger and frustration, and get their book published. The Eight-Step method works!

If you have a comment or question, let me hear from you too. You can reach me at MLevin@aol.com. Good luck!

Martin P. Levin
November 2001

Acknowledgments

The author wishes to express his appreciation to the experts who read the manuscript and made very valuable suggestions:

Jerry Gross, the editor of the revised third edition of *Editors on Editing* and a former associate at New American Library. Jerry lectures at writers workshops. His practical suggestions were very valuable.

Marc Jaffe, an experienced and distinguished paperback and hardcover editor. During his long tenure as editor-in-chief at Bantam Books, Marc helped create and edited some of America's most successful authors. Marc now has his own imprint at Houghton Mifflin and lectures at many writers workshops.

Kendra Marcus, a successful agent for children's books who, with great insight, made many valuable suggestions at an early stage and just before the manuscript was submitted.

Gene Winnick and Evan Marshall, two outstanding literary agents familiar with the New York and international publishing scene.

Robert Halper, Esq., a partner with whom I work very closely at Cowan, Liebowitz & Latman, PC. For the last eighteen years we have worked on many deals together. He made many valuable suggestions throughout the manuscript.

Baila H. Celedonia, Esq., a partner at Cowan, Liebowitz & Latman, PC, who brought her special expertise to bear on the copyright areas of the manuscript.

Maureen Sheehan, Esq., counsel at Primedia, a publishing conglomerate. Maureen formerly worked with me on developing author-publisher contracts.

Holly Brady and Della van Heyst, Directors of the Stanford Professional Publishing Course, who have been generous in allowing me to teach at Palo Alto for the last seventeen years.

Special thanks also go to:

A terrific author of fiction and nonfiction for young people, Marcia Levin, my wife. She read the manuscript with a sharp pencil many times. Her many valuable suggestions and changes allowed my voice to come through.

Claire Hamner Matturro, who worked side by side with me in creating the "Best Bets" section and in polishing this revised edition. No author has ever had a better editor, researcher, and friend.

And without whom this book would never have appeared:

Phil Wood, the unique and independent founder of Ten Speed Press, and the publisher of Ten Speed Press, Kirsty Melville.

Introduction

How would you like help from a literary agent who is in tune with the constantly changing landscapes of publishing, who would read your book before it is submitted to an editor, provide encouragement and advice to you in making changes, map out a marketing strategy for selling your book, and help you prepare an effective proposal for submission to the right editor in the right publishing house? And then after you have sold your book, how would you like a publishing lawyer to help you negotiate the business terms and review the publisher's contract? This book will lead you through all the steps from concept to contract so you can get your book published.

Realistically, experienced literary agents will not represent unpublished authors. And often publishing lawyers are hard to find and expensive to hire. The promise of this book, *Be Your Own Literary Agent*, is that you can be your own literary agent successfully.

As an experienced publisher and now a publishing lawyer, I know you can *Be Your Own Literary Agent*. I have been involved in publishing for half a century. For thirty-four years, I worked closely with agents and authors as a publishing executive. I bought books on my own and later supervised editorial acquisition programs, spending over hundreds of millions of dollars for publishing rights. I was involved in buying fiction and nonfiction, adult and juvenile, hardcover and paperback, and popular and professional books. And for the last eighteen years, as an agent and publishing lawyer, I have worked with authors in developing best-selling books, negotiating their contracts, and getting public attention for their books.

One of the myths in book publishing is that authors, especially first-time authors, need an agent to represent them. Before writing this book, to test its premise, I conducted a survey of editors who are currently receiving unsolicited manuscripts. They reported that when the manuscript is worthwhile and properly presented, they do acquire books from unagented authors. The rejection rate for unsolicited manuscripts is so high, they said, not because the authors are unagented but because most of the books they receive are not professionally written or presented.

Finally, prior to publication, I submitted this book to senior editorial executives and agents. They read what you are about to read. They added their wisdom to what I had written and agreed that if you follow the advice in this book you can *Be Your Own Literary Agent* and be successfully published.

While I was writing this book, I visualized you sitting in my office. I wrote this book in the same style I use when I talk to a client. As you read *Be Your Own Literary Agent,* imagine me at your side. (I recognize that there are two genders. I have used "her" as a pronoun for the author and editor, and "him" for the agent and publisher. I hope you will accept this and appreciate the intention to be representative of my readers.)

I will encourage you to continue, despite setbacks, to write for publication, and I'll share with you stories of how authors such as Tom Clancy, Pat Conroy, and many other rich and famous writers sold their first books without an agent (Chapter 1). I will advise you, if you are receiving rejection letters, how you can find someone to help you improve your manuscript so that you will be able to submit your best work (Chapter 2). I will share with you my "Eight-Step Program for Selling Your Book," and describe every element of this plan in detail (Chapters 3 and 4).

I will introduce you to editors who will tell you what to include in your proposal, how your submission will be judged, how soon you will hear from them, and who will provide a score of other tips to improve the odds of having your proposal read and accepted (Chapter 5). I will describe the rules for creating an effective proposal and illustrate them with over thirty pages of model query letters, cover letters, summaries, sample chapters, and bios. You will be able to compare your own work to the models and make improvements, if needed, before you submit your proposal (Chapters 6 and 7).

Assuming your success in finding a publisher, I will sit by your side as you negotiate the business terms of your contract, comparing it to what, based on my experience, is a "bad," a "fair," and a "good" deal. Then, as I do with my class in Publishing Law at New York Law School, I will help you become contract literate, explaining the copyright provisions and the legal terms you will find in a "standard" publisher's contract, paragraph by paragraph (Chapters 8, 9, and 10).

Along the way, there may be strange terms or unfamiliar techniques. At the back of the book is a Tool Kit that contains a glossary of terms; step-by-step instructions on how to use *Literary Market Place (LMP)*, the agent's primary reference tool; and a list of smaller publishers who are more likely to read and buy your manuscript. You will also find that most publishers have Web pages that will tell you the types of books they are seeking and how to present your book to them.

When we have completed our time together, you will be able to *Be Your Own Literary Agent*. No one can promise to sell your book. Literary agents do not sell every book they offer. What I can promise is that you will have all the information you need to *Be Your Own Literary Agent* and that the odds in favor of selling your book on your own will be better than ever before.

By following the advice in this book, you will be able to present your book to the right editor at the right publishing house as professionally as any agent. You will write, talk, think, and act like a professional author and agent. When you respond to an offer from an editor, you will do so knowledgeably. When you and your lawyer negotiate your contract, you will know what to expect.

I consider this book not only a benefit to you, the author, but of equal service to editors. Editors must discover and develop new authors. The editors who responded to the survey told us that they have, despite incredible odds, discovered and successfully published books submitted by unpublished authors without an agent. My hope is that soon it will be *your* book the editor finds and publishes, and that it is successful . . . and that the time we spend together in the following pages helps to make this possible.

A special word of appreciation is due to the thousands of readers who have purchased the previous editions and to the hundreds who have shared their stories of how this book helped them become a published author.

Good luck.
Martin P. Levin

1

Selling the First Book:
Stories of the Rich and Famous

Although it is regrettable that most agents are not available to the unpublished writer, literally thousands of authors have sold their first book on their own. You can take courage from the knowledge that some of the authors whom you probably know very well sold their first book without an agent.

Consider the events surrounding Tom Clancy and his first book, *The Hunt for Red October*, which he wrote during his spare time while working in his family's insurance agency. Clancy had written a short article about the MX missile for Naval Institute Press, a technical publisher affiliated with the Naval Academy. He submitted the manuscript of *The Hunt for Red October*, on his own, without an agent, directly to the editor at the Naval Institute Press seeking "a professional opinion" for his novel-in-progress. Luckily, Naval Institute Press had just decided to try publishing fiction and Clancy's novel had a strong nonfiction angle—the pursuit of a renegade silent submarine. *The Hunt for Red October* was accepted without an agent and became Naval Institute's first published work of fiction. Despite a small first printing and a limited sales effort from a publisher naive in the ways of trade publishing, Tom Clancy's hardcover book became a startling success.

After the book gained public notice, Rena Wolner, president of Berkley Books, a major paperback publisher, spotted the book, recognized the uniqueness of the approach and the quality of the writing, and bought not only the paperback rights for *The Hunt for Red October* from Naval Institute Press but the rights to all subsequent books as well. It was only at this point that an agent, Robert Gottlieb, was engaged by Clancy. Gottlieb negotiated a $3 million hardcover/softcover deal with Putnam Berkley. When asked if he was surprised, Clancy says, "I was thunderstruck, dumbfounded, bowled over, amazed. But I was not surprised." Clancy still works one day a week at the insurance office but says, "It is hard to get worked up over a homeowner's policy nowadays." Tom Clancy is now an industry with ten mega-seller mysteries, and another ten nonfiction books, software, and games. He is the leading author on the Penguin Putnam list.

Sudden success for unagented authors also happens in the nonfiction field. Robert Coles was a young Air Force doctor stationed in Mississippi in the late 1950s. He was a pediatrician with additional training in child psychology. Peter Davison, an editor at Little, Brown, was impressed by his first article, "A Young Psychiatrist Looks at His Profession," which appeared in *Atlantic Monthly* in 1959. He contacted Coles to see if he'd like to write a book on the subject. That first book led to more than fifty others, which range from studies of children (two of which won the Pulitzer Prize) to biographies and books of selected essays. Modestly, Robert Coles explains that while he does not have "the novelist's gift . . . I have that set of mind . . . and the novelist's sensibility: to show, not to tell." He has handled all these publishing deals without an agent.

One of the most charming stories of discovery concerns Pat Conroy, author of the very successful *The Prince of Tides* and four other novels. While most authors would be pleased to have one book made into a motion picture, Conroy has had three: *The Prince of Tides*, *The Great Santini*, and *The Water Is Wide* (made into the film *Conrack*). Pat Conroy (hard to believe but true) self-published his first book, *The Boo*. Conroy tells the story:

> I went to Willie Shepherd at the People's Bank of Beaufort and said, "Willie, I've written this book about the Citadel and I would like to borrow some money to get it published." He said, "Sure, Bubba, how much do you need?" I said, "Fifteen hundred dollars." He gave it to me. So I thought I had discovered the secret of getting your books published. I said to myself, "This is easier than I thought. I think I will be a writer."

When Conroy finished his next book, *The Water Is Wide*, an autobiographical work about teaching underprivileged black children on Dawfuskie Island off the South Carolina coast, Willie Shepherd could not finance the book. Someone suggested Conroy call Julian Bach, a distinguished agent in New York City. When he called Bach, Conroy recalls, the agent said, "I am so tired of people like you who call me every day. I don't know why I am talking to you. Send it up and I'll read it when I get some time."

The manuscript was in longhand. Since he could not type, Conroy enlisted the help of his friends in Beaufort, each of whom typed one chapter over the weekend on whatever paper was available. The final manuscript was on a variety of paper, long and short, lined and unlined, hard and onionskin.

Some time later, Julian Bach called Conroy. The conversation, as recollected by Conroy, went like this:

> **Bach:** Pat, Houghton Mifflin, one of the oldest publishing companies, wants to publish your book. Here's the really good part, $7,500.
>
> **Conroy:** Julian, I don't think Willie Shepherd down at the People's Bank is going to lend me $7,500.
>
> **Bach:** Pat, you realize *they* pay *you* the money?

Conroy learned quickly, but before he would allow Julian Bach to represent him, he wrote, "Dear Mr. Bach: Who are you? I never heard of you. You're an agent? What exactly do you do? Have you ever done this work before?"

Julian Bach responded and Conroy now remembers sheepishly that Bach provided a history of his agency with a client list that included the estate of Charles Dickens and authors such as John Fowles, the distinguished novelist, and Theodore White, the best-selling writer of nonfiction.

As evidence that unagented first books can be sold in genres other than adult fiction and nonfiction, author and illustrator Patricia Polacco published her fifteenth children's book in April 1993. She sold her first book on her own. Ms. Polacco's professional publishing career began in 1987, when she was forty-one. She had always created artistic greeting cards for friends to celebrate occasions. A friend encouraged her to form a local chapter of the Society of Children's Book Writers and Illustrators. For about a year she prepared work to share with the group. Ms. Polacco said to her friends, "The whole experience set my pants on fire, and I realized, 'By golly, I think maybe I am going to do this for real.'" Shortly thereafter, in 1987, accompanied by her mother and carrying an eighty-pound portfolio, she saw sixteen publishers in one week and sold her first book, *Meteor*, which is still in print.

Scratch an author and a story of the struggle to get a start emerges. There is always that first published article, novel, children's book, or book of poetry. In the beginning, you must realize, none of the great or not-so-great authors spring full-grown from Minerva's brow or are welcomed by publishers with open arms into the literary fraternity. They trod the road you will tread—as an unagented author in search of a publisher. They succeeded and you will too.

In the process, these now successful authors suffered rejections, which are an upsetting part of the publishing experience. For example, the poetry of e. e. cummings was rejected more than a dozen times until it was finally published by his mother. Irving Stone's first book, *Lust for Life*, the story of Vincent Van Gogh, has now sold about twenty million copies. But it was rejected by Knopf (they never even opened the parcel) and fifteen other publishers before it was published by Doubleday. Stephen King, currently America's most prolific and successful contemporary author, had seven novels rejected before *Carrie* was published by Doubleday.

In 1964, a book that added a concept and a phrase to the American language, *The Peter Principle: Why Things Always Go Wrong*, was rejected by McGraw-Hill. The editor's letter said, "I see no commercial possibilities for such a book and can consequently offer no encouragement." Thirty publishers rejected the book until William Morrow adventurously paid $2,500 for the manuscript and printed ten thousand copies. The book sold more than two hundred thousand copies in its first year, remained on the best-seller list for a year, and has been translated into thirty-eight languages.

Not a Day Goes By, a steamy best-selling novel about friendship and love by author E. Lynn Harris, is another recent example of the confident writer who got started without an agent. His sixth novel, *Not a Day* hit the number one slot in August 2000, with well over 212,000 copies in print after four press runs. Yet before Harris hit best-seller status, he self-published and sold his books from the trunk of his car at beauty salons patronized by African Americans. Doubleday published *Not a Day Goes By*.

Other notable success stories of authors who persevered without the initial help of an agent include:

- *The Celestine Prophecy*, by James Redfield, who published the book and sold 100,000 copies before Warner acquired it for $800,000. *The Celestine Prophecy* has sold more than 5.5 million copies.

- *When I Am an Old Woman I Shall Wear Purple*, by Sandra Haldeman Martz, has been reprinted forty-two times, with 1.5 million copies sold.

- Before he was a household name, John Grisham sold copies of his first book, the self-published *A Time to Kill*, out of the trunk of his car.
- Richard Paul Evans wrote, published, and promoted *The Christmas Box*, which Simon & Schuster bought for $4.2 million. It was also made into a television movie.

There are thousands* of stories like this of rejection and success. All of them have several common themes. In every instance, there is an author who is determined to write, to be published, and to reach an audience. Harlan Ellison, the novelist who in three decades of work has had forty-five books and fourteen hundred stories, essays, articles, and columns published, says, "There are the poor damaged souls who must write, who haven't any more choice in the matter than whether or not they breathe." In most instances, the author has adhered to the admonition to retain her full-time day job before making writing a career. Sometimes the writers have been teachers, not necessarily of writing, and worked in a nurturing environment that provided time to build a writing career.

In 1974, New American Library acquired paperback rights to *Carrie*, Stephen King's first published novel, from Doubleday for $400,000, half of which was to be paid to the author. King learned about this on Mother's Day and rushed out to the local drug store and bought his wife, Tabby, a hairdryer, hardly an extravagant gift but all that was available in Bangor. In his memoir, *On Writing*, Stephen King describes the scene when he told Tabby of the sale.

---

*If, after rejection, you wish to have your ego restored, I suggest reading Stephen King's memoir, *On Writing* (Scribner, 2000); *Writing for Your Life*, edited by Sybil Steinberg (Pushcart Press, 1992); and *On Being a Writer*, edited by Bill Strickland (published by Writer's Digest, reprinted in paperback in 1992). And for fun, also read *Rotten Rejections*, edited by André Bernard (Pushcart Press, 1990). This book contains over one hundred letters of rejections written to authors who later became world famous.

I took her by the shoulders. I told her about the paperback sale. She didn't appear to understand. I told her again. Tabby looked over my shoulder at our shitty little four-room apartment, just as I had, and began to cry.

As chairman of New American Library (NAL), one of the leading hardcover-paperback publishers, I was the host at a lunch in King's honor. I sat next to his wife, Tabby, and asked her, "What does this first major money mean to you and Stephen?" She replied, "I hope Steve can stop teaching and concentrate on writing." And so he did.

These are but a few of the war stories that authors tell of their early struggles. You, as they did, must show determination, read voraciously, and continue writing.

However you are occupied now, if writing is your passion and you have the talent and tenacity, you, like thousands before you, will find a publisher. Talent alone is not enough. Sometimes the tenacious get there faster than those with more talent and less tenacity. Be encouraged and stay positive. Selling your first book takes knowledge, which this book will provide. It also takes a strong ego to withstand rejection and persevere. Remember, the editor who rejects your manuscript is not rejecting you but your work, and is challenging you to make it better. You need an editor, but remember, she needs you as well. The discovery of a new publishable author is a coup for an editor, whose advancement depends on her eye for spotting new talent and developing them into publishable authors. The author-editor relationship is symbiotic—each is nourished by the other. Every author, no matter how successful she is now, had to find a publisher for her first book. Find the editor who needs you as much as you need her, and you become a self-agented, published author.

2

Making Your Book the Best It Can Be

The most important talent of a good agent (and the trait you must develop) is his ability to look at a work dispassionately and determine if, in his opinion, it is publishable. The reason some publishers will only read agented books is that they depend upon the editorial savvy of the agent, who acts as a screening device. Spouses and significant others can advise you on many things, but the quality of your work and the efficacy of your presentation to the publisher is outside their field of competence, and they often lack objectivity. As your own agent, you must find outside counsel to reinforce or revise your judgment that the work you are submitting to the publisher is of sufficient quality to encourage the editor to read your proposal and your sample chapter, and then become excited by your work.

There are many ways to get this counsel, starting with an internal checklist. Ask yourself: Is the subject or the theme of the book one in which I believe passionately? Is it an original concept, or at least a fresh approach to an established theme? Is it a subject that I know enough about to make an interesting and useful book? Is there a need for this book? How many people will be interested in my idea? Is there enough depth for a book, or is it a magazine article? (A book, unlike an article, must have scope and sufficient well-developed detail, which adds significantly to the reader's information and enjoyment.) If you can answer "yes" to these questions, all else being equal, you should be able to write a substantial and salable book and, with a professional marketing plan and proposal, sell it to a publisher.

In Chapter 5, you will be taken behind the closed doors of publishing houses, introduced to editors who are likely to read your manuscript, and listen to them discuss their criteria for a book they are likely to acquire. As you will see, the overwhelming response from the editorial assistants who read unsolicited manuscripts is about the lack of quality and professionalism in the submissions.

One of the most common faults I have seen over the years is the attempt by the novice author to seek out an idea "that has never been done before." If the idea has not been done before (and this is doubtful), there is probably a good reason for it. A first-time author, or one who wishes to move her career along, is better served by writing a more intriguing mystery, a well-developed romance, or a better how-to book. The most exciting example of "doing it better" is Martha Stewart, who is now an industry unto herself with seven published books, a cooking school, a magazine bearing her name, and a television career.

Martha was the wife of Andrew Stewart, who worked with me at the Times Mirror publishing group. She is a superb cook, and she loves crafts, antiques, gardening, and entertaining. When I first met her, she was a stockbroker facing a layoff because of declining business in the brokerage house for which she worked. During her downtime, Martha wrote a book called *Entertaining*, which combined fresh and delicious recipes and excellent illustrations with beautiful, creative ideas on being a good hostess. She tested all the recipes in her own kitchen, supervised the photography, and wrote about how to present the right foods in the right social setting. She convinced Crown Publishers to publish her first book, which has now sold over five hundred thousand copies and has continued to create a veritable library of her best-selling books in this genre.

Martha Stewart moved into a crowded field, but she was passionate about her love for food and entertaining. She had an innovative approach, knew her subject in depth, knew that millions of people cared about the subjects she chose, and knew that she could interest them in her work.

Shari Lewis, who died in August 1998 at sixty-five years of age, was passionate about her love for children, songs, and stories. Her career began when she was very young and her husband, publisher Jeremy Tarcher, encouraged her during their honeymoon to write a book she had sold on the basis of a title—*How to Pull Strings and Influence Puppets.* (Shari began her professional career as a puppeteer after having been sidelined from her dancing career by an injury.)

Shari wrote sixty children's books. She was an Emmy Award–winning children's television star. From the beginning, with scores of books, tapes, records, and videos to her credit, Shari was her own agent. I knew Shari and published some of her early books, always dealing directly with her. She was an effective agent for her own work. She once said, "For writers in particular, I think the best advice anyone can give is to be critical about your work until you're done."

Before you expose your book to professional editors, do a reality check of your own. Find published books in a genre similar to yours and ask yourself, "Is what I have written as good as this published book, or better?" This is the first level of the reality check. If you feel you can improve your sample chapter, do it before you submit it to a publisher. Some writers will submit a manuscript saying, "I know this needs work, but I thought you could tell me what to do." If you know it needs work, do the work first and submit it with confidence. If you are not sure of the quality, an editor cannot be enthusiastic about reading it. If you feel any part of your sample chapter or presentation can be improved, do so before you submit it. The best way to improve your odds of being accepted is by offering a quality product confidently.

Recently, I was working with a nationally known businessman and his collaborating writer to test the market for a book he wished to write. The concept was outstanding, the outline was good, but the sample chapter was so poorly organized that the material was inaccessible to the reader. The chapter needed a sharper focus that would reveal the excellent concept. I refused to include the sample chapter in the presentation and stopped interviews with major publishers until it was rewritten.

It was amazing that the author, a top-notch chief executive officer who was well-read and had an excellent critical sense, did not know that what he had written was not publishable. The poor judgment of the professional writer and collaborator was even more amazing. Somehow, writers believe that a brilliant concept will override shoddy work. Not so. To be successful in the highly competitive arena of publishing, you must be the best you can be. Quality counts.

You may not be able to write well enough to win a Pulitzer Prize, but with help and practice you can write a professionally competent manuscript. Find a writers group in your neighborhood or attend a conference. Your local community college or nearby university is a good place to look for such writers groups. Call the English department of the college or university for leads. You may be able to audit creative writing classes for a modest fee. Many adult education programs offer writing classes. The quality may vary, but they will offer you feedback. Check the "community happenings" sections of your local newspaper, and if there is a major bookstore in your area, give it a call or check its bulletin board to locate an appropriate writers group.

If you are part of a writers working group, your fellow writers may be able to provide constructive criticism of your work. Their view of your work may not be the best or most authoritative, but it will help you think about how a reader would react to your work and what needs to be done to improve your manuscript. My research assistant joined such a group at a local community college and reports that at the first session, the group leader warned her that "the problem with us is we like almost everything." Nonetheless, she found meaningful feedback and a helpful sense of community and encouragement.

If you can, spend the time and money to attend a writers workshop where you can get the help of a professional teacher and critic. The *Guide to Writers Conferences* (Shaw Guides, 625 Biltmore Way, Suite 1406, Coral Gables, FL 33134) lists and describes nearly one thousand writers conferences and workshops worldwide. You can also find Shaw Guides on the Internet at Shaw Guides Inc./Writers Conferences and Workshops (http://writing.shawguides.com). The magazine *Poets and Writers*, published by a nonprofit group organized for literary and educational purposes and available in many libraries and quality bookstores, routinely lists information on conferences, retreats, and writing competitions.

Look for a freelance editor or "book doctor." They offer editorial services for a fee. There are twenty pages of names, addresses, and specialties in the doorstop-sized directory of American publishing, *Literary Market Place* (published annually by R. R. Bowker, and available at most libraries). These "doctors," many of whom were former editors of major publishing houses and some retired editors-in-chief, will review your letter, proposal, and sample chapter, and even complete your manuscript for a fee. You can identify the service you want by reading the entries listed in *Literary Market Place* *(LMP)*, in sections labeled Editorial Services and/or Editorial Consultants. You will find descriptions such as:

"analyses of manuscripts"

"manuscript evaluation"

"book proposal development"

These phrases may lead you to the right person to help you. It is important that you and the editor are compatible, if her background is suitable for your project, and if you can afford the fee. Jerry Gross, with whom I worked when he was editor-in-chief of New American Library, has written an excellent, helpful essay, "Working with a Freelance Editor or Book Doctor," which appears in his book, *Editors on Editing*.

Why the emphasis on quality? As an unpublished author or an author unhappy with her progress, you are trying to beat incredible odds in publishing. Publishers receive thousands of manuscripts directly from authors without any solicitation. These are called "unsolicited manuscripts" and are dumped in one place, which has an unfortunate name: the Slush Pile. Not even a Las Vegas bookmaker would quote the odds on an unsolicited manuscript being removed from the Slush Pile and being read, let alone being accepted. You must do all you can to avoid this fate. But take heart: many of the unsolicited and unagented books that pour in to publishers *are* read, usually in a rush. You will increase your chances of having your manuscript read by looking at the publisher's Web site. Many publishers list rules for submitting a manuscript.

Before you expose yourself to this risky, long, and difficult process, the quality of your work should be the very best it can be. Self-analysis, writers groups, retreats, and outside help do not guarantee success, but they will improve the odds, making you more confident of the quality of your work, and thus more persistent in seeking a publisher, because you will have been advised that your book is publishable. After you become a published author, your editor will suggest the direction you should take in your next work and provide the criticism you need to be even more successful.

Once having achieved a professionally competent manuscript, follow the Eight-Step Program discussed in the next chapter. These steps will improve the odds that your manuscript can avoid the Slush Pile, will be read, and will be accepted for publication.

3

The Eight-Step Program for Selling Your Book

It is difficult to shift gears from being the creative artist to being the seller of one's work, but this is a part of the real-life experience of a first-time author. *Literary Market Place* has more than two hundred pages of publishers' listings. Recent government and private studies estimate more than thirty-six hundred publishers in the United States publish three or more books annually. The challenge remains

- to develop a selling strategy,
- to find the right publisher and the right editor,
- and to negotiate a successful deal, finalized by a fair contract.

If you follow this eight-step program, you can sell your own book—successfully. Here is an overview of the program.

1. **Write a Winning Proposal.** A winning proposal is one that will attract attention and present your work in the best possible light.

   In Hollywood, screenwriters make their "pitch" to potential producers in person. They generate interest by presenting a "high concept," a shorthand form of telling the story in an intriguing manner in one or two sentences, hopefully eliciting interest in hearing the story in its entirety. Once the studio is attracted to the idea, the writer is asked to present a short summary and, if acceptable, is engaged to write the screenplay. With a few variations, this is the same basic process that is used in publishing. Your cover letter to the editor must contain a "high concept," crisply stated in a sentence or two, which introduces a carefully crafted proposal that includes a summary of your book, one or two sample chapters, and, for nonfiction, a table of contents. This technique is discussed in Chapter 6, and a wide variety of sample letters and proposals is provided in Chapter 7.

2. Find the Best Publisher. Publishers specialize—even conglomerates (the super-publishers) separate the company into separate divisions and imprints, some devoted to specialized areas of publishing. For example, an author with a romance novel probably would and should seek out Harlequin, the world's largest publisher of romance novels. However, since romance novels now comprise almost half of all popular mass market literature sold, many other publishers are in the market, including New American Library, Warner, Pocket, Bantam, Berkley, Avon, Dell, and Zebra Books. All publish romance novels. There are also smaller publishers, such as Leisure, that buy romance novels. You increase your odds of being published by identifying publishers who are most likely to be interested in the subject of your manuscript. How can you find these publishers?

Literary Market Place is the most authoritative source to help you match your book to a potential publisher. Its weakness is its lack of subjective opinion, a fault remedied by *Writer's Market*, published annually by Writer's Digest Books. This is a good source of publisher listings (although not so extensive—about nine hundred), and includes extra information valuable to the first-time author, such as how often the house buys unagented works, range of advances, and so on. Jeff Herman's *Insider's Guide to Book Editors, Publishers, and Literary Agents* (updated annually) is also good; its chief advantage is its listings of individual editors (and their areas of expertise) at several hundred of the larger trade houses, and a detailed description of each publisher. The 2000 edition has a thousand pages listing editors at over five hundred publishing houses. Herman also has separate sections for university publishers and religious publishers. How to find the *right* publisher is addressed more fully in Chapter 4.

3. Submit Your Book to the Right Editor.   This is by far the most difficult task. While some publishers announce they will not accept unagented manuscripts, the survey I conducted reveals that editors at most of these houses will take a peek at unagented works. Not much of a peek, but a peek. Write to the editor by name. In a recent lecture at the Stanford Professional Publishing Course, at which I teach each year, a leading editor said, "If an author takes the trouble to find out about me and writes a personal letter to me, I will respond." I would surmise that many dedicated editors feel the same way. Besides, all editors dream of finding a new best-seller in an unsolicited manuscript. In Chapter 5, I describe in detail how to find the right editor—and what she does when the manuscript is received.

4. Use the Two P's—Patience and Persistence.   Once the proposal is in the mail, there is an anxious waiting period which is usually longer than the author expects. Our survey, reported in Chapter 5, tells you "What Goes on Behind Closed Doors." Once a suitable time has passed, a follow-up, which *might* send someone to the Slush Pile to find your buried letter, outline, and sample chapter, is in order.

Publishers rarely review unsolicited manuscripts on a regular schedule. Suitable time may mean as little as thirty days and as long as six months—and these delays require persistence and patience. A follow-up after sixty days is appropriate.

5. **Use the Rejection Profitably.** In some instances, the rejected manuscript is accompanied by a form letter. If the form letter has a signature, this is a contact to be exploited. Editors will occasionally talk to authors of unsolicited manuscripts. Sometimes when they reject a manuscript, editors write a *real* letter with helpful comments. A long rejection letter can often shed light on why your manuscript is not being bought. In either case, when you receive a rejection letter with an editor's name shown, you have made progress in finding someone who might discuss your manuscript with you.

  If you can reach the editor who read your submission, the questions you might ask are:

- If I improve the work as you suggested, is this the type of manuscript that your house might publish?
- What are your editorial guidelines? (Before asking this, look for the publisher's homepage on the Internet. The guidelines might be there.)
- If this book is not suitable for your house, do you have suggestions as to who might be a publisher in this area?
- Do you have the name of someone at a house that is publishing in this area to whom I can write?
- Was the proposal inviting? Are there areas I could improve?
- Did the sample chapter(s) effectively display my ability and professionalism?
- Is there someone I could contact who might be able to work with me?

• Is there an agent whom you could recommend who might take me as a client? May I use your name as a reference?

If you are fortunate enough to get a "glowing" rejection, one in which the editor says that you "show promise," follow up and ask the editor, "Do you have any specific suggestions that would help me make my book good enough for you to acquire it?"

6. Keep Moving. Network. Find Places in Which You Can Make Contact with Publishers and Editors. Since you are trying to move from being Mr. or Ms. Anonymous to being a real person in the world of publishing, you need to make contact with real publishers and editors. As was mentioned previously, hundreds of conferences, workshops, and seminars are sponsored by colleges, universities, libraries, and cultural organizations. Normally these conferences extend from two to four days and are attended by aspiring writers or published authors who are looking for current information about trends, editors, and marketing tips. The faculty for these conferences are working professionals from large and small publishers, editors, agents, or established authors. Some of the writers conferences also offer individual critical appraisal of attendees' works-in-progress. The fees vary according to the length of the conference and range from $100 to $400 or more. Try to find a conference close to your home and one that you can afford.

If you cannot attend a workshop, there are writers organizations that conduct regular meetings and provide networking opportunities. You can often find leads on such organizations through your local community college, through advertisements in writers magazines such as *Poets and Writers*, and from the Internet. For example, fiction writers can locate romance or mystery writers organizations and other specialized writing organizations with state chapters with a key word Internet search. Such writers organizations usually have nominal fees, meet locally or regionally, and are designed to support and encourage the writer.

For published writers or other serious writers who find it difficult to write with the distractions of their current environment, there are residences and retreats. These places are not elegant. The rooms are sparsely furnished and inexpensive. There are common halls for meals and meetings where you can make contacts. (Many retreats require the applicant to submit a sample of published work or work-in-progress.)

The *Guide to Writers Conferences*, mentioned previously, is the book that lists all these opportunities. In it, you will find descriptions of the available programs, schedules, faculty credentials, application requirements, living facilities, and costs—all well presented.

Beyond this, you should attend, if possible, the annual trade show of the Book Expo America (BEA). It is held each year, usually at the end of May or the beginning of June, and almost every publisher in America attends. At this trade show, you will see the books publishers are offering for the upcoming fall season and some previously published books. In a single location, you get a sense of what each publisher has on his list. You will get a good picture of where your book might fit on that list. Many editors attend the BEA, and if you are polite and persistent you might be able to get a few moments of conversation. Even more important, the BEA trade show is attended by hundreds of smaller publishers, where you can meet the owner or the publisher— the real decision makers in these companies.

If you cannot afford to visit the BEA trade show, which rotates among Chicago, New York, and Los Angeles, you should attend one of the regional exhibitions that are held in cities throughout the United States. Fewer

publishers attend, but the regional shows have all the benefits, on a smaller scale, of the BEA. (The smaller size will
also increase your chances of personal contact.) All of these
exhibitions and their locations are listed in *Publishers
Weekly*, the trade magazine of the book industry, well
before the event. *Publishers Weekly* is available at many
large libraries and at larger bookstores. It also has a Web
site, www.publishersweekly.com.

7. **Think Small.** Do not be afraid to consider alternatives to
one of the large New York publishers. Some of your best
chances of having your manuscript read by a decision maker
are with a small publisher, many of whom are located outside
New York City. Many of these "small" publishers, because
they have been willing to read unsolicited manuscripts and
work with first-time authors, have become medium-sized,
profitable, and admired in the profession. As I've mentioned
previously, there are more than thirty-six hundred trade publishers in the United States. Most literary agents concentrate,
for obvious reasons (mainly financial), on the largest two
dozen publishers. Consequently, small and midsized publishers work with unagented authors for three main reasons:
(1) they cannot pay the money for advances that the big publishers can; (2) the Big Book/Big Author Syndrome is not as
important to them; and (3) they have to—they'd never find
enough books within their budget to publish if they didn't.

To assist you, I have created a personal list of Best Bets—
small and midsized publishers where your chances of being
noticed and talking to an editor, or even the publisher himself,
are greater than at the major houses (see Appendix C). You
will find scores of publishers listed. You can add publishers to
this list through your own experience. Since addresses may
change, check with the latest edition of *LMP* or call before
mailing material. Small and midsized publishers who value

new authors will read unsolicited manuscripts, and they are more likely to risk publishing a first-time author. Think small. There is time, if you feel it is necessary, after your first published book, to think big.

8. Keep Reading.   Being a writer and an agent is a continuing effort, and you should do what literary agents do: read *Publishers Weekly (PW)* every week. It is the "bible" for the publishing industry. Publishers advertise and *PW* extensively reviews forthcoming books, which will give you a sense of what is coming to the market and of developing trends. Major personnel changes are reported; this information updates the entries in *LMP* so your letter will be properly addressed. And, from time to time, there are excellent articles that describe the market for each of the categories of publishing. Current and back issues of *Publishers Weekly* can be found in most public libraries.

For general background on the publishing scene, read the *New York Times Book Review*, *Time*, or *Newsweek*, or the book review section that appears in your local newspaper. *Writer's Digest* is a monthly magazine that regularly runs updated market reports and frequently lists publishers, editors, and agents and what they're looking for.

The Eight-Step Program
for Selling Your Book

To recap:

1. Write a Winning Proposal.

2. Find the Best Publisher.

3. Submit Your Book to the Right Editor.

4. Use the Two P's—Patience and Persistence.

5. Use the Rejection Profitably.

6. Keep Moving. Network. Make Contacts.

7. Think Small.

8. Keep Reading.

The effective, professional, full-time agent helps his client by using this eight-step program, but he may not know it. He slips easily into these eight steps: he helps his client write or improve her proposal; he knows, or thinks he knows, the right publisher and editor to get a sympathetic reading and he knows how long to wait before following up. If there is a rejection, the agent seeks the editor's advice for improvement. Where indicated, agents will make submissions to midsized and small publishers if they believe they can get a more sympathetic reading of the manuscript there. A good agent is always on the move, keeps up to date, and knows the specialized publishers who might buy the book he is selling. When you follow this eight-step program, you will be doing everything the professional agent does to sell his client's book. With practice, you might even do it better.

4

Finding the Best Publisher for Your Book

The publishing industry has become very complex over the last four decades. Hardcover publishers own mass market houses. Publishers of professional books also publish trade books. Almost all publishers create what the industry calls trade paperbacks, a softcover version of the hardcover book. About half of all mass market paperback books never appear in hardcover, but are published as paperback originals. Each type of book dictates a different submission strategy. Use this chapter as a road map to lead you to the category in which your book would fall.

1. The Trade Book
2. The Mass Market Paperback
3. The Juvenile Book
4. The Professional Book
5. The Scholarly and University Press Book
6. The Subscription Reference Book
7. The Elementary or High School Textbook
8. The College Textbook
9. The Religious Book

Once you find the category in which your manuscript falls, you are on the way to finding the best publisher for your book.

To find the right publisher, you need a clear picture of how publishing is organized—and to understand how complex it has become. While there may be exceptions, publishers fall into these basic categories.

The Trade Book

Trade books are hardcover books and trade paperbacks (the larger full-sized paperback, not the rack-sized mass market ones) designed for the general consumer and sold for the most part in bookstores. Public libraries are also major customers for trade books. In some instances trade books are sold to libraries and schools for classroom use. Many trade book houses have juvenile divisions, publishing hardcover and paperback books for children.

Included in the trade book category are books of fiction, non-fiction, biography, classics, cooking, history, popular science, travel, and art. You will also find trade books that help in learning a foreign language and "how to" books that guide the reader in participating in sports, music, poetry, and drama. The categories of nonfiction books are virtually limitless.

Some book publishers have a narrow focus. Generally speaking, the smaller the publisher, the tighter the focus. Fodor's (a subsidiary of Random House) has a narrow focus selling only travel books. But most of the largest trade book publishers produce fiction and non-fiction books, hardcover and trade paperbacks, adult and juvenile books. The names of these trade book companies are well known, and most of them are deeply involved in more than one area of publishing. The goliaths of trade publishing are Random House, Harper-Collins, Penguin Putnam, Simon & Schuster, Warner/Little, Brown, and the complex of St. Martin's/Holt/Farrar, Straus & Giroux—

these trade publishers account for almost two-thirds of all trade books sold in the United States.

Trade paperback books, once a rarity, have become a staple of the industry, and virtually every hardcover house publishes them. They are usually the same size or slightly smaller than the original or hardcover editions, unlike the much smaller mass market paperbacks. Trade paperbacks are sold primarily in bookstores, but are often sold wherever hardcover books are sold. Because of the popularity of the format, trade paperbacks vary in size and are designated "trade paperbacks" chiefly due to their specialized content and higher prices. Their sales and distribution practices and returns policies adhere to those of their hardcover brethren, not their mass market relatives.

To determine whether a particular trade publishing house publishes books in your genre, conduct research in the following six sources.

1. **Use *LMP*.** You can start by consulting *Literary Market Place*, which lists every publisher, large and small. In *LMP* there is (1) an alphabetical listing of publishers (which includes the names of executives and editors for each house) and (2) a list of publishers by subject area. Use the alphabetical and category lists to find a specific publisher. If you are interested in locating a publisher of juvenile books, for instance, *LMP*'s category index provides a list of all publishers of "Juvenile and Young Adult Books." Here you will find, for example, Harper-Collins listed as a publisher in this category. You would then look up HarperCollins in the alphabetical index located in the front section of *LMP* to get the address, telephone number, fax number and e-mail address for HarperCollins. There you will also find the names of the publisher, editorial directors, and editors. The listing in *LMP* also provides the number of titles in print and the annual number of titles published. This

can be used to measure publishing activity. The date the company was founded, which measures its longevity and possibly its stability, is also shown. You should be able to find the house you seek and the name of an editor to whom you can write. Be aware, though, that editors move from publisher to publisher, so call and check *before* sending your manuscript.

The list of potential publishers for your book will probably be too large initially, and you should refine the list by following steps 2 through 6.

2. **Write for a Catalog.**   Once you have finished your initial search, write to the address shown in *LMP,* attention "Customer Service," asking for a catalog of new and backlisted titles. Almost all publishers have a homepage on the Internet, and you can order a catalog on line. Some publishers even maintain online catalogs you can study on the Internet without the delay or expense of ordering one. By studying the catalog, you will get a feel for whether or not the book you are writing (or have written) would fit into the publisher's program. This should enable you to eliminate some of the names you found in *LMP* and narrow your target list.

3. **Visit a Library, Bookstore, or Trade Show.**   Visit your library (if you are not already there using *LMP*) or a bookstore, where you can find the books published by a house that you believe may be a potential buyer of your manuscript. Visit a bookstore, especially a "superstore" owned by an independent bookseller, where from fifty thousand to one hundred thousand titles from all publishers will be on display. If it is a quiet time in the bookstore, a knowledgeable clerk can tell you a great deal about the publisher and his books. And since most bookstores are organized by categories, the shelves will contain most of the current published books in the genre in which you are interested. Check to see

which publishers have books in your category. If you attend the BEA or any other trade show, you will also be able to see the books publishers plan to release in the next season. This investigation will give you an excellent idea if your book is likely to be of interest to a specific publisher.

4. **Try to Meet a Publisher's Sales Representative.** If you are very lucky when you are at the bookstore, you might run into the salesperson for the publisher. (You are more likely to find him at a trade show.) The sales "rep" is an excellent source of information for you. He can tell you if your book fits within the category of the books his house publishes. He knows his list and his competitors' lists, and which books and categories sell. If asked, the "rep" might be able to give you the name of the editor to whom you should send your proposal, and he can provide valuable insight as to the books his publisher is likely to accept.

5. **Check *Books in Print*.** All nonfiction (and fiction) books are listed in the annual directory *Books in Print*. Most libraries have *Books in Print* in the reference section. A check of the listings will reveal those books similar to your book, and who published them. This is a valuable tool—especially the Subject Guide, which will help you find the titles of published books that might compete with your manuscript. There are volumes of *Books in Print* that list paperback books and forthcoming books, and provide book reviews. *Books in Print* can often be accessed from your home computer through large public and university library Web sites. And a comparable search for similar books in and out of print, sometimes with more detail than *Books in Print*, can be conducted online through amazon.com.

When you compare your manuscript to books already published, you can determine how your book differs. Most editors who read nonfiction manuscripts are impressed when you tell them how your book compares with books previously published—it shows you've done a professional job of researching the competition and the market for your book, and will cast you in a favorable light.

6. Find the Right Editor.   At the end of this process, you should have created a list of publishers in your category, narrowed them down, studied their lists, and obtained the address and name of the appropriate editor to whom to write from the listing in *LMP.* (Another method: check the acknowledgments in a book you feel is similar to your book. More often than not, an author will thank her editor by name.)

Always write to a specific editor. Since publishing is known for its high turnover rate, you might find it difficult with limited knowledge to select the right editor. If you write to the wrong or a long-gone editor, your proposal will usually be forwarded to the correct editor, but why take that chance? It's best always to confirm information by phone. Ask the editorial assistant who is likely to answer the phone if your contact name is correct and, if not, who the person is who edits books like yours.

Your objective is to send your proposal to the *right* editor at the *right* publishing house. Each of these steps increases your odds of success.

The Mass Market Paperback

Since over 50 percent of all mass market paperbacks are books originally written for paperback publication without a prior hardcover publication, this is a significant market for authors. Proposals for books that are likely to be published as "paperback originals" should be submitted directly to the paperback publisher. However, the market has become complicated since gradually, over the last two decades, most of the larger hardcover publishers have acquired or developed their own mass market paperback companies. The following are several examples:

Bantam, Dell, and Random House have a single owner, Bertelsmann. Each of these companies has independent editorial departments, but each will buy hardcover and paperback rights for their own lists.

HarperCollins, a venerable trade publisher, has its own mass market paperback entity, Harper Paperbacks, and has recently acquired Avon (paperback) and the William Morrow Company (hardcover, trade paperback, and juvenile books).

Penguin Putnam (hardcover, paperback), New American Library (hardcover, paperback), Dutton (hardcover, trade paperback), and Viking (hardcover) are owned by Pearson, Ltd. and operate as Penguin USA, with one executive directing all the subsidiaries and divisions, each of which has a great deal of independence and separate editorial departments.

Putnam Publishing Group publishes an extensive line of hardcover and trade paperbacks under the Putnam, Grosset, and Jeremy P. Tarcher imprints. Putnam also publishes mass market books under the Berkley banner, and how-to and children's books under the Price Stern Sloan, Grosset & Dunlap, and Putnam imprints. Each entity acquires books independently.

Random House owns the mass market paperback houses Ballantine, Fawcett, and Del Rey, a science fiction line. Here, too, the paperback publishers have separate editorial departments.

Simon & Schuster, a diversified trade publisher with a major presence, owns Pocket Books (paperbacks) and Collier Books (trade paperbacks). In addition, Simon & Schuster has a wide variety of imprints with separate editorial departments.

St. Martin's Press publishes hardcover, trade paperback, and mass market titles in many subject areas. It also owns Tor Books.

Time Warner, with major interests in magazines and books, owns Warner Books, which publishes in hardcover, trade paperback, and mass market, and Little, Brown, which is a hardcover and trade paperback publisher.

Zebra Books and its recent acquisition, Pinnacle Books, publish a large list of mass market originals and occasional hardcover and trade titles.

In submitting a manuscript to those publishers with both hardcover and paperback divisions, you should submit your book to the hardcover imprint, unless it is the type of book that is rarely published in hardcover—for example, romance novels, westerns, or travel books. In most instances, the hardcover publisher will endeavor to buy hardcover, trade paperback, and mass paperback rights. Alternatively, when the hardcover publisher feels he can get a larger sum of money for paperback rights by selling them to another company, he will retain the rights and sell them, after hardcover publication, to the highest bidder for paperback publication.

A first-time author submitting a book to the largest houses (those that publish about 70 percent of the titles in the trade and mass market areas) must be careful to select the right subsidiary or division, and then identify the editor to whom the book should be submitted. *LMP* will help because it lists the imprints (divisions within a publishing house) and the editors of each imprint, but, if you are in doubt about which imprint to approach, call the publisher's promotion department. If you are lucky, one of the assistants will explain the organizational structure. Then, look for the name of the editor shown in *LMP* and call to verify the listing. The question "Does Miss Brown still edit mysteries?" will probably get you the information you need.

The Juvenile Book

The juvenile book market is a $1 billion plus market in sales. Many trade book companies have a line of juvenile books and acquire these books in the same manner that they acquire trade books. Agents usually represent established authors. Unpublished authors submit their manuscripts directly to the publisher. Illustrators are often represented by agents, but some are independent and carry their work around in portfolios to show editors, when they can get an appointment. There are many literary agents who represent authors of juvenile books, and there are a few agents such as Kendra Marcus of BookStop, located in the San Francisco area, who deal exclusively in children's books worldwide.

One of the main factors in the juvenile book boom is the growth of publishers that specialize in this market. Scholastic is a very large publisher of juvenile books in a variety of formats. They publish hardcover and paperback books that are sold to schools and the trade, have book clubs for schools, operate book fairs, and supplement their books with films and audio. Scholastic is now the dominant juvenile publisher in the United States and in many foreign countries. Scholastic is also the U.S. publisher of the Harry Potter books.

Selling your manuscript in the juvenile market is similar to selling your book to a trade publisher. If you follow the six steps for trade books as described above, you will be able to find the best publisher and the right editor for your juvenile manuscript. While significant improvement has occurred in royalty advances paid to the more popular authors and illustrators, the economic terms offered to a majority of the writers of children's books are significantly less than those offered to writers of adult books. What encourages writers to accept less in advance payments is that the life of a juvenile book is usually far longer than that of an adult book. For those who have the talent, writing for children is still rich and rewarding. Publishers for the juvenile market are often accessible to you without an agent.

The Professional Book

The professional book market is not as complex as the trade market
and editors are far more accessible. In this field of publishers, there
are three major subdivisions:

1. **Technical and Scientific Books,** which include subjects in
   technology, engineering, and the physical, biological, earth,
   and social sciences. These books are directed at practicing
   and research scientists, engineers, architects, and other professionals in these fields.
2. **Medical Books,** written for physicians, nurses, dentists,
   hospital administrators, and others in human and allied
   health services.
3. **Business and Other Professional Books,** addressed to
   business people, managers, accountants, lawyers, librarians,
   and other professionals.

Several traditional business publishers have broadened the business
category, once restricted to serious professional literature, and now
also produce nonfiction books for the general reader, some of which
have become commercially successful. Doubleday and Harper-
Collins both have divisions specializing in popular business books.
Your research, as described in the trade book section above, will
locate all those professional publishers who cater to readers of popular business books.

Unlike trade books, where books are created entirely by outside
authors, manuscripts in the traditional professional areas are sometimes originated in house (by the publisher) and developed with the
help of outside writers.

In other areas of professional publishing, such as medicine and
engineering, for example, authors are sought by editors called "acquisition editors," who attend professional meetings and visit campuses

to meet authorities in the field and seek out their manuscripts. Many books are developed from unsolicited manuscripts. An author with an idea for a book in the area of her expertise can usually find an acquisition editor at a convention or meeting who will arrange to review a manuscript. Failing this, she can submit a query letter to the professional publisher's editor-in-chief, who would be listed in *LMP.* Most professionals know the leading publishing houses intimately, since much of their professional reading is published by them. In general, editors in the professional and scientific areas of publishing are often accessible by telephone, especially to professionals, and they are more responsive than editors in the trade areas. The size of this market is substantial; while served by fewer publishers, on a dollar-volume basis this area of publishing is roughly equal to the revenues of all trade books. Professional books are not as glamorous as trade books, but they are important to professionals in the United States and throughout the world.

As an illustration of these principles, Dr. Elizabeth Berger, a medical doctor, wrote in March 1999 to tell me she had "found a publisher on my own by following your 'sage advice.'" Her book, *Raising Children with Character,* was published by Jason Aronson, Inc., a publisher of professional books. Dr. Berger appeared on *The Today Show* and is now establishing her own Web site.

The Scholarly and University Press Book

While some scholarly books are published by not-for-profit entities, research institutes, museums, and learned societies, some university press publishers are publishers of choice for professional and trade books. Their excellent editors often have one eye on the general trade as well as the scholarly market. There are over one hundred university presses, most of which are members of the American Association

of University Presses (AAUP). The largest of the university presses—
Harvard, Yale, MIT, University of Chicago, Johns Hopkins—have
recently become an excellent alternative for authors of serious trade
books. This phenomenon has occurred because many of the traditional trade book publishers are publishing fewer serious nonfiction
books. Nonetheless, even the aggressive, trade-oriented university
presses still publish primarily for the scholarly market. They are a
good market for the serious book that may have popular appeal, especially if the hardcover book would ultimately find its way into a trade
paperback list, which university presses have and treasure.

LMP lists all of the university presses, along with their editors.
However, the Association of American University Presses publishes
a more extensive directory with a list of editors and other useful
information.*

While university presses and other scholarly publishers do not
represent a large market, they are ideal for the book that is designed
for a specialized, serious market, and occasionally for a trade book
that will sell to a professional college audience.

University presses maintain a sales staff that sells to university
bookstores as well as to general bookstores. When university presses
have a book with trade potential, they publish and sell it in much the
same manner as a commercial trade publisher.

The Subscription Reference Book

Encyclopedias and other reference books have been a major force in
publishing, with distinguished sets of books that have been created
and revised over the years. Many articles are contributed by writers

---

*This directory, which is issued annually, is extraordinarily valuable because it is filled
with useful information to help the author submit her manuscript. You can find this
book in most libraries or purchase a copy from the Association of American University Presses, Inc., 71 W. 23rd Street, New York, NY 10010, or by calling 212-989-
1010 or faxing 212-989-0275. The AAUP also has a Web site, www.aaupnet.org.

with special expertise in their field. Since the domestic hardcover market for these books has been shrinking, and more work has been moved inside to the salaried staff, this represents a limited and less attractive market for the freelance writer.

The Elementary and High School Textbook

Books serving the elementary and high school markets represent billions of dollars in sales annually. These books are created by a limited number of publishers, all of which are listed in *LMP.* The major publishers, such as Pearson Education, McGraw Hill, Houghton Mifflin, and Harcourt control this market. The books and materials are generated internally, often with the help of freelancers.

In creating a textbook for the elementary–high school (El-Hi) market, the publisher, with his staff and expert consultants, sets out a concept or framework for a series of books to be created in a discipline along with supplementary materials to be used in the classroom. Materials for computers, which are becoming more common in schools, are also included in the package to enhance the learning experience.

The publisher then seeks authors who can create the books in the program. These are usually teachers or curriculum specialists who have demonstrated the ability to communicate to the student. Publishers seek out these writers by visiting schools, attending conventions of teachers, and reading the professional press. Authors with educational credentials who have the ability to write books in a manner appropriate for the grade level are sought. Some authors of El-Hi texts are paid modest royalties; most work on a flat-fee basis in which the author receives a fixed payment for her work, without any royalties, on completion of the assignment. For the qualified author, this is an interesting and lucrative market. Rarely is there a need for an author with credentials to use an agent to sell her work.

Some publishers have contracted with outside editorial "packagers" who, following the individual publisher's guidelines, create the entire "package"—text, illustrations, software, and promotion materials. These "packagers" are prospects for the nonfiction writer with a background in the subject. You can find these companies listed in *LMP* under "Book Producers."

A far better market for the writer with the skills to write for student audiences is the publisher who develops supplementary books— juvenile books designed to supplement the El-Hi textbook in the classroom. Some of the leading companies in this field are Greenhaven Press, Chelsea House, and Lerner. While the authors' earnings are modest, the supplementary books often stay in print for a long period of time and produce steady royalties. The books are written for the El-Hi student, sometimes heavily illustrated (provided separately by the publisher), and are curriculum related. While *LMP* lists the publishers who develop supplementary books, they are more readily identified by visiting a library with a good children's book collection, or by visiting the semiannual American Library Association trade show and the International Reading Association Trade Show. It helps to see firsthand who publishes the kind of books you wish to write rather than just looking at a catalog and a list of publishers. *PW* announces when and where these trade shows take place.

The elementary and high school market is one of several markets that can provide income, experience, and writing credits that are helpful on a curriculum vitae. The writer usually works on a freelance basis under the term of employment "work for hire." This legal term covers the arrangement in which the publisher asks the writer to write a specific piece under his supervision and directions. The writer is usually paid a one-time fee and occasionally a modest royalty. Copyright is held by the publisher, who owns all rights to the book. Working on projects under the direction of a publisher may generate opportunities for the writer of original works to publish them with a division of that publishing house that concentrates on trade juvenile books.

The College Textbook

College publishing is also a major specialized market, changing now with the growing importance of the computer. Textbooks, for the most part, come from experts in each field. Recently, publishers have created the "managed textbook" in which the publisher sets out the framework for the book and seeks authors to write some or all of the contents. As in the case of El-Hi books, authors are recruited by acquisition editors who read the appropriate literature, attend conventions, and visit schools. Authors need educational credentials (usually a Ph.D.) and must be respected in their field. It is a market limited to the professionals.

An author who feels she has the educational qualifications and something special to offer should send a query letter to the publisher. If the publisher is interested in the subject proposed by the author, she would, as in trade book publishing, follow with a book proposal: a summary, a table of contents, a sample chapter, and a curriculum vitae. The publisher will usually expect the author to do an analysis of the competitive texts in the field to help him make a decision. Unlike trade publishers, the college publisher is usually responsive to a prospective author's inquiry for two reasons: (1) professional courtesy and (2) a belief that the potential writer, who is usually a professor, might have influence in adopting the books she offers. Rarely does a college text author use or need an agent, and rarely is an advance or royalty important to the author. The prestige associated with a published textbook and the requirements of the profession to "publish or perish" weight the scales in favor of the publisher, who may even require that the author provide illustrations at her own expense.

The Religious Book

Included in this publishing area are Bibles, hymnals, and prayer books as well as many other types of books. These days, this market is not limited to the professional theologian. Many religious houses publish inspirational books of all kinds, including fiction, nonfiction, and poetry, and constitute an excellent market for the qualified author. The tools and techniques for determining the publishers in the market for inspirational books are the same as for trade books.

The market for religious books has broadened. Previously the domain of the denominational houses such as the Baptist Publishing House or the Paulist Press, trade publishing houses have entered the field and the traditional religious publishers have also expanded their lists.

Thomas Nelson, a Nashville-based publisher, is typical of the religious publisher who now provides new opportunities for authors who can write for the inspirational audience. Nelson grew from a small Bible business into a major factor in religious book and music publishing when it acquired Word, a Dallas-based publisher. The Nelson list is dotted with luminaries such as Dale Evans, but also has a place for the new author with an inspirational story to tell.

"Angel books" have become, at least for the present, religious book best-sellers. One publishing house, Barton & Brett Publishers, Inc., was actually founded to publish *Where Angels Walk*, written by a newly discovered author, Joan Wester Anderson. This book became a major best-seller in hardcover and then in paperback. This and other books created a new category in the religious field and has led to successful careers for authors who never before enjoyed major success.

An excellent source for identifying a potential market, such as the religious and inspirational market, is to find a spring or fall books issue of *Publishers Weekly* at your super-bookstore or in a local library. This issue of *PW* lists over twenty-five hundred books to be published in the forthcoming season. In a recent fall book issue there were thirty-four different publishers who announced new books. By reviewing the lists of forthcoming books organized by category and publisher, you can discover emerging trends and the little-known publishers who may be your best market.

What the Future Holds

The author looking to the future must take note of the e-book. Individual sales of this electronic book have been modest. Nevertheless, the modern author clearly must become familiar with e-book publishing as she may find this an avenue that will enable her to be published directly on the Internet. When Stephen King published a book, *Ride the Bullet*, directly on the Internet without the sponsorship of a publisher and sold 600,000 copies, a new market was born.

Publishers Weekly now has regular, continuing coverage of the e-book phenomenon. You should follow the development carefully as this may be a way for you to reach a market directly and attract the attention of a publisher for the print version. The Writers Guild's Web page also contains articles about e-book publishing, and at least one recent article warned prospective authors about the risks in some e-book publishing contracts.

Find your place within this publishing framework and make a series of inquiries until you find the most likely publishers for your book and the editors to whom you should send your proposal. This overview of publishing should help you realize that you have many publishing options, more than you first imagined; your publisher of choice might be other than a traditional trade publisher. With an understanding of the book industry and its areas of concentration, you can improve your targeting and find the *right* publisher for your book. A careful canvass might find a market for your book you might otherwise have overlooked. Remember: hunting for the right publisher is best done using a rifle rather than a shotgun.

5

What Goes On
Behind Closed Doors

Who is that mysterious and crucial person, the editor, who will receive your manuscript, and what happens once she has it? Will she just send it back unopened? Will she peek at it to be sure she is not missing a valuable book? How much will she read? Will she respond to you? How long will it take before she responds? If she thinks your book is publishable, how will you be informed?

In order to determine the current conditions of play, and to help finalize the recommendations on how to draft your proposal, I interviewed a representative number of editors. This chapter, in large part, is based on their responses.

In general, *most publishers accept unsolicited manuscripts*. Some editors who said they do not accept unsolicited manuscripts admit that when they receive one they take a peek; if the manuscript is intriguing, they will read the submission before they return it, and sometimes ask for more material. Almost all publishers will read a short query letter that identifies the subject and tone of the book you hope to submit. Many publishers use their Web pages to encourage submissions.

Smaller publishers and university presses are generally the most receptive, and larger publishers the least receptive, to unsolicited manuscripts. Some publishers, such as those who publish romance novels and children's books, look forward to receiving unsolicited manuscripts. *It is a myth that a publisher will not accept unsolicited manuscripts.* Certainly, there are a few major houses, inundated with author mail, that will only read agented manuscripts, but if you select publishers carefully and write to a specific editor, your manuscript can get in the front door of most publishing houses. Interesting side-light: one of the largest and most prestigious trade publishers reported that all editorial assistants meet every three weeks and are treated to a pizza lunch as they read their way through unsolicited submissions. This is a tradition originated by the founders of the firm who, when they started, personally read every manuscript submitted.

The quantity of unsolicited manuscripts varies in direct proportion to the size of the publisher, and the estimates we received in the survey ranged from five to two hundred a week. One very successful mid-sized publisher, who said it was a tradition for him to read unsolicited manuscripts, commented that "every year the volume increases and the quality decreases." The challenge for you is to develop and exhibit your skill, talent, and professionalism in every way so you will be noticed and distinguished from the poorly prepared submissions.

My survey revealed that the person who reviews a manuscript is not always a low-level reader. In some houses, especially where the submission is directed to an editor by name, the editor herself reads the proposal (once again, the moral: write to the editor by name). In other instances and more commonly, it is an editorial assistant, a junior editor with limited experience, who is the reader. In a few instances, publishers use freelance readers. A most interesting finding was that in one small prestigious publishing house with respect for new talent, the editor-in-chief herself, whenever possible, looked through the unsolicited manuscripts. Many respondents reported that searching through the Slush Pile is like "looking for a needle in a haystack," but they still looked.

When we asked how much of the manuscript was read, the most frequent response was the first chapter or less. (Tip: get off to a fast and strong start.) Some said they read the first chapter and skimmed the rest; another respondent said she could tell the quality of the manuscript by reading the first ten pages. Some publishers said they read only the cover letter and the beginning and end of the manuscript. (Tip: keep it short.) Given the large influx of manuscripts and limited resources available, it is not surprising that very little of the manuscript is read. For this reason you should *never submit a completed manuscript*, but should send one or two sample chapters, along with a proposal, that will excite and intrigue a harried and overworked reader.

Only veteran authors or those fortunate enough to write a highly successful first novel can sell their next work of fiction with just a summary or outline. If your outline is intriguing, the editor will encourage you to complete the book. With few exceptions, a novel must be complete before a contract is offered; too many first-timers have started wonderfully but sputtered badly before finishing. An aspiring writer must prove she can finish the job.

The advantage of writing nonfiction, however, is that the book is rarely finished (most are barely begun) at the time of acquisition. The qualities of nonfiction writing are more easily judged. If a first-timer can write a smooth sample chapter, a convincing proposal, and a detailed chapter outline, the odds are that she can write the rest of the book in similar fashion. (One of the points of the proposal, however, should be to convince the editor that the book is all but written.) As a matter of fact, I advise against finishing a work of nonfiction. Normally a good editor can make constructive suggestions before you complete the manuscript.

The bad news is generally conveyed in writing. In most instances, the author is informed of a negative decision by a form letter. One publisher's form letter suggests that the author find an agent by consulting *LMP*. Some houses will modify the basic form letter; others have a variety of form letters. The turnaround time is generally from six to eight weeks. A few houses respond in a month, but the author should be prepared for a long wait for a response. Publishers understand that authors are likely to make multiple submissions. However, they like to be informed if the manuscript is being sent to other publishers. (Some submission guidelines note that simultaneous submissions are allowed, but the query letter should note this. A few guidelines note that simultaneous submissions are not permitted. Check the guidelines at the publisher's Web site, or check for submission guidelines in such sources as *Writer's Market*, or write or e-mail for guidelines if this is an issue.) Practically all publishers insist on a self-addressed stamped envelope (SASE) large enough to accommodate the manuscript. (A new practice of submitting a SASE sized and stamped for only responsive correspondence, with a notice in the query letter that sample pages should be recycled instead of returned, can save you some return postage and envelope problems; some submission guidelines even encourage this practice. Almost all submission guidelines warn you that the publisher is not responsible for the safety of materials, so never send originals.) If the SASE is omitted, you risk not getting any response at all.

We asked editors what happens when they read a manuscript that has merit. Some said they discussed the manuscript with others in the editorial department. After the discussion, they might write a letter with specific suggestions, and many said they would talk to the author on the telephone (so include your telephone number in your letter). In some instances, the reader would write a letter of general encouragement and ask to see more of your work, or if this was not a book in their area of interest, they would suggest other publishers who might be interested.

When we asked the editors what the chances were for a manuscript to move from the status of unsolicited manuscript to the point of serious consideration, the news was not very encouraging. The responses read:

> "Once in a blue moon"
> "Not very many make it"
> "Accepted nothing in ten years" (another said nothing in
>   twenty years)
> "Small percentage"
> "Two out of fifteen referred on, but they are ultimately
>   rejected by the editor"

"One in a million" (another said one in a thousand—that
    is better)
"Five to ten percent"
"One or two a year"

The odds of the unsolicited manuscript moving to the stage where it
will be read and possibly accepted are not great. Mostly this is due to
the number of submissions received, the limited resources available to
screen the manuscripts, and the poor quality of most submissions.
This discourages some publishers from investing staff time in what
they believe is an activity with a low return. You can beat these odds
if you use every skill at your command.

I asked the editors who reviewed unsolicited manuscripts for
suggestions that could be passed on to you.

One editor suggested that you talk to an editor (who might
be at a writers conference, for example) before starting the book
and get advice as to the areas of interest of the publisher and the
market served by the publisher. It would be fortuitous if the book
you write fits into the publisher's "wish list." The same editor suggested a visit to bookstores to assess the market and avoid direct
competition with well-established books (although there is almost
always room for something better). Others suggested that you
study publishers' lists to make sure the book you submit fits into
their interests. These suggestions were repeated many times by
other editors.

Respondents repeatedly (and somewhat naively) suggested that
the first-time author get an agent, especially for fiction. This was a
common suggestion because, as an executive editor of a major publisher said, she expected the agent to "winnow" out the bad material.
But many respondents went on to give helpful suggestions as to how
to submit books directly to the publisher. The editors interviewed
generally said they preferred a cover letter, a synopsis, a first and second chapter, and a bio. A query letter before submitting a proposal
is useful, some said, especially for nonfiction.

When we asked the editors if they accept telephone calls, the responses were mixed. Some said "yes"; some said "no"; some said "no" with an exclamation mark—and others said "it depends." This is an area in which the first-time author should proceed with caution. A phone call is more appropriate if an author has received a letter with encouraging words from the editor.

Another editor suggested that the first-time author get feedback from someone other than a family member. Another said, "Do not make the package so difficult to open." One of the most dedicated of the editors in the business was a joy. She said she had been looking for nonfiction books about dogs (no wonder: *The Hidden Life of Dogs* by Elizabeth Marshall Thomas, published by Houghton Mifflin, was a big best-seller in 1993). And she also said, "It is *very* exciting to get a good unsolicited manuscript." With her dedication, it is no wonder that she discovered a book in the Slush Pile. It was *Lily*, a western love story by Cindy Donner, which she published successfully and which was made into an MGM film.

This was not the only success story that emerged from the survey. *Thinkertoys*, a book about creativity in business by Michael Michalko, was an unsolicited manuscript and became a major book, with foreign rights and book club sales. At another publishing house, *Car Pool*, a light, funny murder mystery by Mary Ghill, was discovered by an editorial assistant who subsequently worked closely with the author to make the book publishable. Not only was the author successfully published, but the editorial assistant, as a result of her work with the author, was promoted to associate editor. And still another publisher reported that *Sudie*, a novel by Sara Flanagan, was discovered in the Slush Pile and published successfully with paperback, TV movie, and foreign rights sales. These are just a few of the titles and authors discovered by publishers who regard reading unsolicited manuscripts a necessary part of their function.

While the odds of success are not great, the editors tell us that if the author has a quality book that is skillfully presented, it will rise up out of the Slush Pile to be recognized. One editor remarked that

Judy Blume, the prolific teenage-fiction writer who broke new ground in the field, was discovered in the Slush Pile. The discovery of a best-selling author does not happen often, but if it happens just once, publishers are encouraged to accept and read unsolicited manuscripts. Your challenge is to make your submission superior so that it will set you apart from the "slush" in the Slush Pile.

What Makes an Editor
Select a Book

What makes an editor select a book? Gerald Gross's book, *Editors on Editing*, asked this question. Astute and respected editor Richard Marek answered the question brilliantly. I had the good fortune to work for many years with Marek and when we worked together, he discovered the late Robert Ludlum, the best-selling author. Marek helped him become one of the most successful authors of spy fiction.

In his essay in *Editors on Editing*, Marek describes the editorial decision-making process. Marek says there are three kinds of books. First is the sales department book, which is more likely to be sought by the sales manager than the editor—"always nonfiction, fills a market need and is easily explained to the buyer."

The second kind, according to Marek, is the genre book: mysteries, romances, thrillers, "women's novels," gothics, histories. These are books that generate income from the sale of subsidiary rights. The reprint rights to these books are purchased by paperback houses and book clubs. (In view of today's market, where many of these categories go directly into paperback, this must be modified.)

The third category is the "editor's" book, which does not fall into any of the genres, but is acquired because of the author's "feel and passion." Such a book is *Jonathan Livingston Seagull*. Peter Mayer acquired the paperback rights when he was publisher at Avon Books for $1 million, at that time a record-breaking sum. It was a huge success. Who, other than such a talented editor, would have thought an illustrated inspirational book about a seagull would sell millions of copies in paperback?

Today in this multimedia world, editors, in selecting books, also look at the promotional possibilities of the book and the author. Is the author one who could do well on *Oprah*?

Marek says that, in reading a manuscript, he looks for something he has not seen before—a new idea, a new voice—"the jolt one feels at the unexpected." Books that epitomize this concept, Marek says, are *Moby Dick* by Herman Melville and the works of J. D. Salinger. It is asking a great deal for you to reach those heights—but it makes the point.

In fiction, Marek listens for the voice of the writer. He asks himself, "Do I wish to spend the next several hours with the author? Do I trust him? Is he entertaining? Does he render familiar scenes in ways that are new, or unfamiliar ones in ways that make me see them clearly? Does he reveal enough of himself to make me like his company?"

After voice, there is pace. Is it a page-turner? In Ludlum, Marek explains, "Events move with the speed of a bullet."

Then there is character. "Do we *like* the characters? Do we care about their fates? Do we have an emotional investment in whether they marry or divorce, revenge themselves on those who did them wrong? Do they live? Are they complicated, surprising, *real*?" Marek says that if the answer is "yes" to these questions, the editor will be strongly influenced to buy the book.

Fourth is the plot. The story must draw us along because "we want to know what happens next, and whether what happens next convincingly surprises us. Arbitrary surprises won't do. Logical ones are glorious."

Next comes style. Marek says that "good writing is a lovely thing in and of itself, but it isn't enough to make me want to take on a book."

Finally, there is verisimilitude—not accuracy, but "if the author convinces me it's true, I don't care if it really is true or not."

For the first-time author of fiction, to meet these criteria is a major challenge, but it is what an editor seeks when she searches through the Slush Pile.

In nonfiction, the elements are the same but the priority is different. Marek puts voice first: "The reader must trust the author." The "hack" who presents his "groundbreaking" conclusion without logic is a loser.

Second is subject matter, though it might well be first instead. Subjects vary because tastes change. However, as reinforced by television fare, it seems "sex, money, murder, bizarre relationships, and the kinks of the rich and famous tend to be perennially popular." While Marek did not mention this, an excellent indicator of the perennially popular subject is *Reader's Digest*. Study several years of back issues, and the all-time favorite subjects of its readers are the nonfiction subjects listed on its covers.

Third, Marek looks at the organization of the material. "One wants to be led by an expert. The author sure of his facts, and selecting them wisely, is likely to convince us of his expertise."

Fourth, there is style. "The author who writes well can make even an unlikely subject seem interesting." John McPhee made Alaska fascinating, and more recently, Elizabeth Marshall Thomas made *The Hidden Life of Dogs* so accessible that it became a major best-seller.

Finally, as in fiction, there is verisimilitude. Marek writes, "Recently I read a book on something I really don't believe in: reincarnation. Yet the author made me believe that *he* believed and I read the book avidly, troubled and confused."

The technique of identifying a publisher and preparing an attractive proposal is not enough in itself. Richard Marek, speaking for all editors, has defined what editors look for in a manuscript. The quality of the writing must shine. His advice is to read what you have written, listen for the voice, check the pace, live with the characters, review the plot (or in nonfiction, its credibility), study the style, and evaluate the verisimilitude. If you can find and rate these factors in your book on a scale of one to ten—and give yourself a seven to ten—you have a strong chance of attracting the editors who are anxious to find their next best-selling author.

6

The Book Proposal:
Where the Author and Editor Meet

For thirty-four years, I read hundreds of book proposals, and in the last eighteen years, I have helped authors write them. The proposals are as varied as the personalities and subjects of the writers. But every successful proposal has the same qualities and components.

Established writers will submit a short summary of their book—sometimes as short as one $8\frac{1}{2} \times 11$-inch piece of paper—and have the book contract follow. Along with my editors, I have read a one-page story summary and, based on the author's reputation and previous books, authorized a million-dollar advance. The first-time writer does not have this luxury; she is unknown, without a track record, and unlikely to get a megabuck advance—and certainly not on a single-page outline.

Thus, a query letter is a means of determining the interest level of an editor in the subject of your book. The techniques of writing a proposal or query letter are as different as the books presented in them. This chapter will discuss the techniques of writing proposals and query letters. In the next chapter, there are models for you to study and use to develop your own style. But first the principles: the book proposal is designed to sell your book and *yourself*. The book proposal is an "interview" with the editor; it determines whether you get the opportunity you are seeking. So the proposal has to demonstrate your professionalism and your ability to write. A well-written proposal says you can write a publishable book. The query letter is the "invitation to the dance" that should be sufficiently attractive to energize an editor to ask for a proposal or sample chapters.

The Proposal—Rules to Live By

Despite the differences in books, there are some general rules that apply for all book proposals, and because they are so basic, they are discussed first. In her article "What Editors Look For" appearing in Gerald Gross's *Editors on Editing*, Jane von Mehren begins her advice on writing a proposal with these rules. I agree with her rules, and have added some of my own.

The Basics

The Format

1. Letters and all enclosures should be typed. In these days of computers, you have a choice of typefaces. Select a common, readable typeface (at least 10-point, preferably 12-point), then make certain your printer is operating on its best behavior, so the material you submit is dark enough, attractive, and readable. Always use black ink, and never use a dot-matrix printer—letter-quality is best.

2. Use uniform $8^1/_2 \times 11$-inch paper, preferably a good white bond paper. Use normal margins, usually $1^1/_2$ inches on the top and to the left, and 1 inch to the right and on the bottom.

3. Always double-space the summary, or table of contents, and sample chapter. The cover letter and bio can be single-spaced.

4. Identify each part of your proposal by starting a new sheet (e.g., Summary, Table of Contents, Sample Chapter, Bio). Number all pages so that it is easy for the reader to follow.

5. Check spelling and grammar and proofread everything in your proposal. A sloppy manuscript is a turnoff.

6. Avoid fancy headlines or use of exotic type. The proposal should be neat, dignified, and inviting to read.

7. As I've said before, address your submission to a specific person determined by your research.

8. Keep a copy of what you send, including your cover letter.

9. Enclose a self-addressed, stamped envelope (SASE) or mailer if you want your manuscript returned.

10. Always include your name, address, telephone number, and where applicable, fax number.

Once you've covered the basics, determine your strategy. If you are out to locate potential buyers and your subject, usually nonfiction, can be explained in a letter, you might use a query letter to do this.

The Query Letter

The query letter is a pithy, enticing letter from the author to the editor that encourages the editor to ask for more. This technique is used extensively in seeking magazine assignments, where most assignments are for nonfiction articles and where the content can be described readily in a letter of one to two pages (but not much longer). Yours should ideally run one page, get to the point quickly, and persuade the editor to ask to see the rest of your material.

Some book editors in our survey suggested that first-time authors use query letters because it gives the editor a way to respond more quickly and more directly to the book idea presented. The first-time author should use a query letter only for nonfiction. A short, dramatic presentation of a nonfiction concept encourages an editor to ask for a full proposal. The best positive response to a query letter is a request for the author to send in a proposal. The author should have a full-fledged proposal ready to send to an editor who expresses interest in the project. A long hiatus between an expression of interest in response to a query letter and the submission of a proposal might well be counterproductive.

The Book Proposal

The function of the book proposal is to so excite the editor who reads it that she will write, telephone, or fax the author, inviting a discussion that will lead to a contract to publish the book. *Never submit a complete manuscript.* (The only exception to this would be for a juvenile picture book or novel, when the entire story is relatively short.) On the other hand, if you send only a few assorted pages of the manuscript without a summary of the book or information about you, the editor will not understand what she is reading, what your book is saying, or who you are. You have minutes, not hours, of the editor's attention, so use this time judiciously. Create a proposal with four, possibly five, parts to it.

1. The Cover Letter—This, much like a query letter, must:
- make an impact;
- describe the book, including the permissions, illustrations, and photographs needed, and who will provide them;
- define the market;
- evaluate the competition—show how and why your book is either newer, better, needed, more comprehensive, or all of these and more;
- set out the scope of content;
- show why you are the perfect person to write the book;
- estimate the length;
- tell when the book could be completed.

The cover letter must have impact, compelling the editor to read on. Remember, editors are very busy, and are just looking for an excuse to toss your letter aside. Don't give them one.

2. **Summary**—After your cover letter attracts the editor's attention, the summary of the book should draw her into your book proposal. The summary, depending on the complexity, can be from one to ten pages in length, and should set out clearly and in reasonable detail just what the book is about. A good summary, or overview, of a nonfiction book vividly and quickly introduces the book's concept; makes clear the style in which it will be written; shows how and why there is a need for it; defines the book's audience as specifically as possible, both quantitatively and qualitatively; and defines its competition, showing how this book is different and better in some way than other, similar books. For a work of fiction, the proposal can be shorter and simpler, merely describing your novel and giving a short summary of its contents.

3. **The Sample Chapter(s)**—While the summary is a quick synopsis of the book that illustrates your writing skill, the sample chapter(s) should introduce the editor to the essence of your book and your writing style, and make the editor wish she had the rest of the book to read. Most editors want to see the first chapter and possibly a second chapter. Provide only enough *high-quality* material to show the promise of your book.

4. **Table of Contents**—Since the sample chapter is only a sample of the book, you should furnish a table of contents especially for your planned nonfiction book. This is absolutely essential. It demonstrates the scope of the book, and the logic you use in presenting the information to the reader. In many

instances, a detailed chapter-by-chapter breakdown, with one or two paragraphs about the material to be covered in each chapter, is helpful. It tells the editor that you know how to organize the material and that there is enough material to make a book (see pages 76–78 for an example of an expanded table of contents).

5. **The Bio**—If the editor is satisfied with the summary and the sample chapter, the bio should reassure the editor who asks: Can this author really complete this book? Does she have the background or credentials to write a successful book? The editor has heard of untutored, first-time authors who are successful (such as Margaret Mitchell, who only wrote one book, *Gone with the Wind*, which became a best-selling book, won a Pulitzer Prize, and later became the basis for an enduring film), but she is wary. You are an unknown. She needs the comfort of knowing you have life experiences that support the positive feelings she has developed after reading the cover letter, the summary, the sample chapter, and the table of contents. You must assure her that you are the right person to write this book. Anything indicating professional writing experience, or expertise in the subject of your book, should be included.

The author should also describe what she can do to promote the book: contacts with organizations, the media, and colleagues, for instance. Include any media and public speaking experience. If this is lengthy, it may be a section of its own. Publishers love authors who understand the limitations of marketing budgets and who are fully prepared to assist actively in the publicity and promotion of their book. If you propose to promote and demonstrate the book by making personal appearances (for example, for an exercise book), enclose a photograph.

6. **What Not to Include**—For a children's book that you will write but not illustrate, do not include any illustrations. (If your book is accepted, the publisher will find an illustrator for it.) Do not burden your presentation with any other material. The sparse, well-organized presentation is more likely to be read and lead to a request for more material. Send in the entire manuscript only if the text of your children's book or poetry book is just a few pages.

7. **Pulling It All Together**—To organize these elements in your mind and settle on what to include in your book proposal, visualize a group of young editors sitting around a table eating pizza (a real-life situation), and visualize one editor reaching for your proposal. In your mind's eye, look over her shoulder as she selects your package.

   First, she will read your captivating cover letter (one page, two at the most). Second, she will read your excellent summary of the book and be so taken with it that she will wish to read (third) your table of contents (generally nonfiction). Fourth, she will read your sample chapter (or put it in her carry-home bag to read at home) along with your bio, and soon will write or call you with good news.

8. **Do's and Don'ts**—Here are some suggestions that will increase your chances of success.

- *Don't* send in an entire manuscript. Editors have reported that they read only the first ten pages at most. You are better served with a sample chapter.
- *Do* work hard in selecting a title that is a "stopper." A catchy title that succinctly and memorably communicates what your book is about is ideal. If you cannot come up with one, identify your title as a tentative or working title.

- *Don't* try to be an amateur marketer of your book. Let experienced salespeople develop the "selling handle" to be used in presenting the book to a book buyer. You can and should *suggest* how to reach and appeal to your book's market.

- *Do* let others, especially people in the publishing industry, read your proposal. Listen to their suggestions, but accept only those with which you are comfortable.

- *Do* make sure you have appropriate, written permission for the use of material from other books or the names of individuals you are including in your book.

- *Do* look at competitive books, especially if yours is nonfiction, and *do* compare your book realistically (and let's hope, favorably) with those books in your cover letter. If you have or can get the published sales figures for competitive books, *do* include this information as well.

- *Do* follow up after about sixty days, knowing that reading unsolicited manuscripts is a low priority. Try a follow-up letter first and then a telephone call to the assistant to the editor to whom you wrote.

9. **Why This Method Works**—Obviously no one can guarantee that any book proposal system will result in the acceptance of a manuscript. Even experienced literary agents with excellent contacts can't guarantee that a writer's work will be accepted. This method, however, helps you establish relationships with editors, and a good relationship between an editor and an author is precious.

    The editor is in publishing because she delights in finding good books and talented authors, and in seeing her books appear on a publishing list. Aside from the reality that most publishing houses are deluged with manuscripts and never provide sufficient staff to review the Slush Pile, editors prefer to see a book at its earliest stage and prefer a submission by a first-time author in a proposal form. Using a proposal, an editor can evaluate the concept of the book, review the table of contents, read the sample chapter, and then make a meaningful, creative contribution to the book as she shapes it for publication. To discover work from a new author is the dream of every editor. She needs you and you need her. Professionalism on your part can help make this relationship happen.

If you have chosen an attractive book concept, developed it with skill, carefully selected the publishers to whom you submit the work, identified the appropriate editors, prepared the book proposal artfully, and are determined and persistent, you will increase the chances that your book captures the attention of a publisher.

In the following chapter, you will find samples of a query letter, cover letter, summary, table of contents, sample chapter, biography, and finally a complete proposal. In some instances, I drafted these. In other instances, I selected outstanding models submitted by my clients, actual aspiring writers. The models are at a level of excellence you can achieve or exceed. Review these samples carefully and compare them to the quality of what you submit. Make every part of your proposal the best it can be. The competition to get published, both from first-time authors and established writers alike, is fierce. To win, you must use every advantage available.

Models—
Query Letter, Cover Letter, Summary, Table of Contents, Sample Chapter, and Bio

The dual role of an author and agent requires you to be self-critical. To help you, I have selected and, in some instances where material was not available, created models of the components of the proposal: a query letter, a cover letter, a summary, a table of contents (and some variations on the theme), a sample chapter, and a bio. Together these elements should combine to form a persuasive, compelling proposal.

These models and the comments that precede them will help you create and check the quality of your submission. Since your book will be different from the books used in the models, these samples will serve as idea generators and illustrate a level of quality and a format that you can apply to your own proposal.

You will find on the following pages:

- Query Letter—a letter used primarily when publishers do not accept unsolicited manuscripts or when you wish to determine interest from a wide range of potential publishers. Models are for nonfiction and fiction.

- Cover Letter—a letter that accompanies and introduces a full-scale proposal, including a summary, a table of contents, sample chapter, and a bio. Models are for non-fiction and fiction.

- Summary—a condensation of the information in the book. The model is for nonfiction, which also addresses the market and the competition; a longer summary than appears in the cover letter is not necessary for a fiction proposal—better to send an actual sample.

- Table of Contents—a list of the contents by chapter indicating the scope and organization of the book. Models are for nonfiction only and include an expanded version that combines a summary with table of contents.

- Sample Chapter(s)—one or two chapters that indicate the author's style, voice, and quality of writing. Samples are provided for nonfiction and fiction.

- Bio—the author's résumé illustrating the background she brings to the work. Models are presented in résumé form and in paragraph form.

The material in this chapter illustrates each component of an effective proposal, one that is likely to attract the attention of the editor reading unsolicited manuscripts. The material written especially for this chapter is of a level that you can achieve. When you complete your proposal, ask yourself the question, "Does my proposal read as well as the models?" If the answer is "yes," your proposal meets the test.

Query Letter—Nonfiction

A good query letter meets these standards:

- is addressed to a specific editor
- conveys the scope and tone of the book
- is short and to the point
- uses anecdotes to intrigue the editor
- identifies the size of the potential market
- discusses the competition
- estimates the length of the book
- encourages the editor to ask for the full proposal
- encloses a bio
- encloses a self-addressed, stamped envelope

The following sample* covers all these bases in one short page, thereby increasing the likelihood that page will be read and get a positive response.

---

*This is not a real query letter, but one I created as an illustration, using a published book. I am sure that Elizabeth Marshall Thomas could have written a better query letter—as you may know, her book *The Hidden Life of Dogs*, published by Houghton Mifflin, was a #1 best-seller and continues to sell. It has become a classic.

Sample Nonfiction Query Letter

August 16, 1996

Ms. Mary K. Smith
Editor
H&W Publishing
200 Avenue B
Somewhere, PA 11002

Dear Mary K. Smith:

I am an anthropologist and I have always lived with dogs, and I believe behind the wet nose and the wagging tail there is a hidden life. In my book, which I plan to call *The Hidden Life of Dogs,* I will tell about the eleven dogs with whom I have lived.

Readers will meet Misha, a husky who jumped a fence daily and roamed a suburban territory of 160 square miles, and Mara, his true love, who bore his first puppies and then, after he moved away with new owners, gave herself indifferently to any adequate male passerby.

This will be a book about dog consciousness. Humans are not the only beings who have thoughts or emotions. Dogs have thoughts and feelings, they adopt human mannerisms, they make choices, they smile.

The book, although not scientific in nature, will report on what I estimate to be 100,000 hours of observation. This will be a popular book for the millions of dog owners who know that their dog has a hidden life which they wish to understand. As far as I can find, there is no competitive book on the market.

I visualize this as a book of about 144 pages, which I can complete in about one year.

I hope you are sufficiently interested to respond to me so I can send you the table of contents and the first chapter. My bio is enclosed and on it you will find my address and telephone and fax numbers.

Sincerely,

Elizabeth Marshall Thomas

Enclosure (Bio, SASE)

Query Letter—Fiction

The sample fiction query letter is written to a specialized publisher—in this instance, one that publishes romance books. The writer tells enough of the story to interest the editor and explain why she is uniquely qualified to write this book. She has asked for an answer and provided the essential information for a response. The letter meets the following standards:

- is addressed to a specific editor
- identifies the topic of romance
- has an intriguing twist—the Russian locale, which has rarely been written about before
- tells the story in a high-concept form
- sets the estimated length
- states how long it would take to write
- gives the editor the "inspirational ending" of the novel
- establishes the author's qualifications to write the book
- is short and to the point

Sample Fiction Query Letter

Croydon Towers
33 Bleecker Street
New York, NY 10013
Phone: 212-555-1234
Fax: 212-555-4321

September 9, 1996

Ms. Millicent Middlemarch
Editor, Romance Line
Pinnacle Books
1234 S. 21st Street
Philadelphia, PA 23456

Dear Ms. Middlemarch:

Romance abounds in the area of the world that formerly lay behind the Iron Curtain, yet this is undiscovered territory for the romance novel today. I have a file of romance story ideas of loving relationships that were threatened by the harshness of life in these countries. I am preparing to write a series of romance novels utilizing this material.

My first book, *Gorky Street,* which will be about 75,000 words in length, is set in Russia. The heroine is Yulia, the daughter of a famous Russian general, who is forced into a loveless marriage with a KGB official. On a trip to the United States with her father, Yulia, who acts as his English interpreter, falls in love with an American diplomat. Yulia realizes that she must not in any way encourage this relationship.

With the downfall of the Communist Party, her husband and father are stripped of their ranks and benefits. Yulia, because of her English language skills, is sought out and becomes the editor of a popular English-language magazine. She provides the main source of income for her proud father and husband. Yulia learns that she obtained the job because of the American diplomat, who fell in love with her when she was in the United States. He comes to Russia to urge her to leave the hardships and disarray of her native land, divorce her husband, and become his wife.

The chance to go to the United States, to live comfortably, to get out from under the tight control of her father and husband, and to raise a family, is attractive. Yulia agrees to leave and then is tormented by her decision. She elects to stay, make her own country better, be loyal to her father, and build a future with her husband.

Having lived in Moscow with my husband, who was a correspondent for the *New York Times* for three years, I have the background needed to write this story. As you will see in my bio, I have written extensively for magazines. I should be able to complete this in a year.

I hope this concept for a novel will interest you so that I may send you a full proposal.

Sincerely,

Jennifer Jordan

Enclosure (Bio, SASE)

Cover Letter—Nonfiction

The cover letter introduces the editor to the book proposal. This sample* for nonfiction contains the following elements:

- catchy opening paragraph that presents the "high concept," such as "Southern belle survives Civil War but is rejected by her lover" *(Gone with the Wind)*
- a second paragraph that opens the door to the book by identifying some of the specifics to be included
- a description of the "voice" to be used (e.g., nontechnical)
- the length of the book
- a description of the enclosures in the proposal
- the omnipresent SASE

---

*I wrote this letter as a hypothetical illustration from the material found in *Understanding Depression* by Donald F. Klein, M.D., and Paul H. Wender, M.D., published by Oxford University Press, 1993.

Sample Cover Letter for Nonfiction

July 19, 1996

Ms. Mary K. Wang
Editor
Wang & Hill
19 Union Square West
New York, NY 10019

Dear Ms. Wang:

Recent studies have found that one woman in five, and one man in ten, will suffer from depression some time during the course of their lives. This is a disturbing statistic but there is hope, because more and more evidence has surfaced to indicate that many psychiatric disorders are chemical imbalances that can be successfully treated with medication.

Our book, *Understanding Depression,* will be a definitive guide to depressive illness—its causes, course, and signposts, written in terms the lay reader can understand. We will include several self-rating tests in the book enabling the reader to determine whether or not he should seek psychiatric evaluation. We will describe the symptoms of chemical depression (as opposed to nonchemical depression—a more common illness).

The book will be written in human terms and in reader-friendly language, and we will use excerpts from patient histories to show the progress of typical patients and their recovery.

We will discuss the various antidepression medications (including Prozac), and the benefits and side effects of these drugs. This will be a readable guide to this much misunderstood illness. As you are aware, there have been a number of books on the drugs and the illness. Our book will be the most comprehensive book available.

We believe the book will be about 50,000 to 75,000 words and will be completed six months after we get a positive answer from you.

We have included a table of contents, the introduction to the book, and Chapter 1, which we feel is a good sample of our writing style.

Our curricula vitae are included, which will provide you with addresses and telephone numbers at which you can reach us. A self-addressed, stamped envelope is also enclosed.

We look forward to your response.

Donald F. Klein, M.D.
Paul H. Wender, M.D.

Cover Letter—Fiction

The sample cover letter for fiction* has been based on a sequel to the famous Arthur C. Clarke novel, *2001: A Space Odyssey.* This illustration demonstrates an effective but brief cover letter and covers the following bases:

- sets up the premise of the book in "high-concept" style in the first two paragraphs to engage the editor's interest
- provides a title that describes the book
- identifies the enclosures
- explains that this is a multiple submission—with a preference for the publisher to whom it is being submitted

If the cover letter encourages the editor to read further, it has accomplished its purpose.

---

*This description was adapted from the copy contained in the paperback version of Arthur C. Clarke's best-seller, *2001: A Space Odyssey*, published by Signet Books of New American Library, which has sold over three million copies.

Sample Cover Letter for Fiction

Astro House
12 Round Hill Road
Dallas, TX 87674
Telephone: 405-555-7788
Fax: 405-555-8877

Ms. Mary K. Wright
Up and Down Publishing
10 Harbor Drive
Port Chester, NY 10581

Dear Ms. Wright:

My novel is set in the first year of the twenty-third century, the year 2201. The commander of *Discovery,* a spacecraft traveling at a hundred thousand miles an hour, is closing in on its destination, the farthest edge of the solar system. The crew includes a navigator, three deep-freeze hypernauts, and Hal, a chatty computer who guides them.

The mission was set off by a shrinking slab found within the moon's crater Clavius. This is a deliberately buried calling card left by an alien intelligence millions of years ago. And the crew must find answers wherever and whatever they are.

My working title for the novel is *2201: Second Space Odyssey.* I expect it to run between 75,000 and 100,000 words and take about a year to complete.

I am enclosing a plot summary, table of contents, a sample chapter, and an informal bio. Please read on—and call or fax me or write to me at the address shown above. I have enclosed a self-addressed, stamped envelope.

Sincerely,

Arthur C. Clarke

P.S. This is a multiple submission; however, I sense a good fit with Up and Down's science fiction list and am especially interested in your reaction to this proposal.

Summary—Nonfiction

Two crucial parts of the proposal are the summary, or overview, and the sample chapter, preferably the first chapter of the book. A good summary encourages the editor to read the sample chapter. The summary should convey enough about the book to give the editor reading it reason to believe there is enough material for a successful book. Demonstrating the scope and thrust of the book and assuring the editor that the author can write effectively are the primary purposes of the summary. It should also, however, address the market for the book, its competition, and why the book is superior in some way. The sample summary shown for nonfiction is the actual summary submitted by Professor Gerald Gunther, whom I represented, which resulted in the sale of his book, a biography of Learned Hand, to Knopf and then as a paperback to Harvard University Press.

Although Professor Gunther, a constitutional law scholar, wrote the best-selling case book used in constitutional law classes, this was his first trade book and his first major biography. It was necessary that his summary demonstrate his ability to write an engaging biography.

In his opening paragraph, the author established the major premise of his book: the life of jurist Learned Hand. It was necessary, in the beginning, to assure the publisher that this book was not to be a recital of the cases decided by a famous judge, but a personal saga. The author described in detail the sources he was using, including his personal observations as a clerk to Judge Hand.

This exceptional example of a summary for a nonfiction book sets forth the subject, the material, and the author's point of view, and demonstrates the author's ability to write for a general audience. Also touched upon are the market (audience) for the book, and the book's competition (or lack of it).

Sample Nonfiction Summary

LEARNED HAND: THE MAN AND THE JUDGE
(WORKING TITLE)

By Gerald Gunther
William Nelson Cromwell Professor of Law
Stanford Law School

The major purpose of the biography is to explore the distinctive ingredients of the public figure and of the private man; and my central objective is to delineate the interdependence of the public and the private in Learned Hand.

Hand's public career prompts my biography, but it is by no means its exclusive concern. The career was impressive. Although he never sat on the Supreme Court, Hand (1872–1961) was a federal judge for over 50 years, and he is widely regarded as ranking with Holmes and Brandeis and Cardozo in 20th-century American judging. Moreover, his public life was intertwined with some of the main strands of 20th-century political and intellectual developments. For example, in the first decade of the century, he was one of that small group of New York City intellectuals presiding over the birth of *New Republic* magazine; he was an advisor to Theodore Roosevelt in the Progressive movement and indeed ran for public office on the Bull Moose ticket soon after he became a federal judge; and even after his withdrawal from partisan activities after World War I, he maintained close ties (and sustained an extensive correspondence) with figures ranging from Bernard Berenson to Walter Lippmann, Felix Frankfurter, and J. D. Salinger.

But my interest in Hand goes substantially beyond those ingredients of the public image. I am especially intrigued by the complex interrelationship between the private man and the public figure. In Hand's case, there is a wealth of information. Most important is the collection of Learned Hand Papers, a collection of about one hundred thousand items, to which I have exclusive access. (The Papers were given to Harvard Law School on the condition that they remain closed until the biography is done. I am the designated biographer; and the major portions of the Papers are in my possession.) I know of no papers on the 20th century comparable to these in depth, range, and candor. Hand did not like the telephone or dictating to a stenographer; he was more like a 19th- than a 20th-century correspondent in finding it most congenial to record his deepest thoughts via pen and ink and, unlike a John Quincy Adams or a Felix Frankfurter, he did so without any self-conscious sense of history looking over his shoulder.

Hand was an unusually introspective as well as articulate individual, and his correspondence is filled with his reflections not only on the world around him, about political and philosophical and literary and legal issues, but about himself as well. Moreover, I came to know Learned Hand and to spend many hours with him in his last years, after serving as his law clerk in 1953–54. Beyond that, I have interviewed many persons who knew him well.

The special importance of Learned Hand, the public man, lies in the way he executed the task of judging and of dealing with the controversies of a long, tumultuous period in American history. Two models of judging have competed in the endless search for the proper role of the judiciary in our constitutional democracy. One model, the interventionist, activist one, is evaluated (and often admired) largely in terms of the ends it seeks—"justice," "equality," etc. Earl Warren and William O. Douglas are among the modern illustrations of that model. Learned Hand is the best example of the competing, more modest and restrained yet also creative model, a model which assesses judges more in terms of process rather than results. That modest model places the highest value on open-mindedness, detachment, and impartiality in approach, on thorough analysis, and on persuasiveness in reasoning.

I believe that Hand's judicial career is the single strongest datum we have to demonstrate that the modest yet creative model of judging is attainable. Not only does Hand rank with Holmes and Frankfurter as a leading articulator of that model, but his performance on the lower federal courts, more clearly than that of any Supreme Court Justice, illustrates that the model is achievable in real life. To a remarkable degree, Learned Hand managed to behave as the modest judge should.

How did Hand manage it? What accounts for his rare capacity to practice what so many others, not only Hand, have preached? What kind of person could achieve such a rare congruence of theory and practice in judging? Pursuit of these questions is the major aim of my book. Hand's judicial career provides the impetus for examining his life. But a judicial biography, certainly Hand's, must go beyond. Accordingly, a central focus of my study is the human being beneath the judicial robes. That emphasis discloses numerous clues to an understanding of the complex personality that made possible, and perhaps compelled, the perform- ance of the judicial task in Hand's way.

While most sketches of Hand depict him as a magisterial, serene figure, Learned Hand viewed himself as driven by self-doubts and uncertainty for most of his nine decades. Outside observers and the subject himself seemingly pro- duced contradictory portraits; yet there are elements of truth in each: the pre- eminent judge was a product of the driven, self-doubting man, long before he became a judge. Reflectiveness, questioning, skepticism, intolerance of absolutes, a relentless search for answers despite an abiding conviction that there were no permanent ones: these traits emerged gradually in his Albany youth, matured at Harvard, and were cemented in his few years of law practice before ascending the bench. And, most impressively, Hand did not stop doubt- ing, searching, and growing during his long judicial career.

Throughout Hand's life, his reflectiveness and skepticism were entangled with the darker, "can't help" elements of indecisiveness and melancholy. Throughout an increasingly distinguished career, he never ceased doubting the worth of his own work and the justifiability of the mounting applause. The self-doubt permeated all aspects of his life: there was recurrent self-questioning and moodiness and gloom. Yet these dark agonies did not produce intellectual paralysis.

One of the few issues on which Hand held strong convictions was the choice between the models of judging. He believed that the modest, restrained, disinterested role was the only proper one for a judge in a democratic society. It was a conviction nurtured by the teaching of James Bradley Thayer at Harvard Law School and by the abuses of judicial power during the Lochner era in the early decades of the 20th century. Hand's unmatched capacity to behave in practice in accordance with the prescriptions of the modest model was in part a rational, logical deduction from theoretical premises. But in at least equal part, it was a product of sensitivity, wisdom and, above all, another "can't help": the skeptical, doubting, open-minded human being could not help acting that way as a judge.

I view myself as writing for a general audience rather than a predominantly legal one, and I therefore do not plan to discuss his more than three thousand judicial opinions in detail. Rather, I illustrate his manner of deciding cases through a discussion of a number of illustrative clusters, relying on his revealing letters as well as his published and unpublished opinions. In selecting the illustrative areas, I expect to use those of greatest interest, especially those on constitutional questions. Opinions on freedom of political speech, obscenity, copyright, and deportation for lack of "good moral character" are my prime candidates for these discussions. My major concern will be to delineate how Hand's personality and character shaped his public career and his concept of the judicial role. In my discussion of the judicial career, I will emphasize his temper and character (and his political and intellectual environment) rather than the details of legal rules. In this manner, I expect to cast important new light on the judicial philosophy reflected in the frequently reprinted collection of his papers and addresses, *The Spirit of Liberty* (1952) and his Holmes Lectures, *The Bill of Rights* (1958).

I do not believe that there is much need to explicate the contemporary relevance of Learned Hand and his career. The competing models of American constitutional judging—the model of the modest, restrained judge as against that of the activist, interventionist one—stirred debate even during the era of the Framers. That debate pervades our history. The controversy continues today, and will tomorrow. Learned Hand's career is widely considered to be the best modern example of the modest yet creative model, and it is that role of Hand's that largely prompted me to undertake this biography.

Nor do I need to belabor the relevance to humanistic interests of a broad-gauged biography of one of the greatest of America's judges. But the ties between Hand and the humanities go beyond my general theme. For example, at Harvard College in the early 1890s, Hand's major teachers were Josiah Royce and William James and George Santayana, during the Golden Age of Harvard's Philosophy Department. Had it not been for family pressure to join the legal profession, Hand would no doubt have pursued graduate work in philosophy. Beyond that, Hand's life and work constitute an outstanding example of the humanities-oriented judge. I cannot resist concluding with a well-known, especially apt passage from Hand's writings:

I venture to believe that it is important to a judge called upon to pass upon a question of constitutional law, to have at least a bowing acquaintance with Acton and Maitland, with Thucydides, Gibbon and Carlyle, with Homer, Dante, Shakespeare and Machiavelli, Montaigne and Rabelais, with Plato, Bacon, Hume and Kant, as with the books which have been specifically written on the subject. For in such matters everything turns upon the spirit in which he approaches the questions before him. . . . Men do not gather figs off thistles, nor supply institutions from judges whose outlook is limited.

That passage captures a theme at the very core of Hand; its substance echoes throughout his letters and his life.

Table of Contents

Including a table of contents is only necessary, or advisable, in a non-fiction proposal. The purpose of the table of contents is to show the scope of the book, and that the remainder of the book beyond the sample chapter has been well thought out. If the chapter headings are indicative of the content, the editor can visualize how the book will develop.

Lee Iacocca, legendary for rebuilding Chrysler Motors after having been fired from Ford Motor Company after thirty-two years of service, regularly had his hair cut by the same barber at the Waldorf-Astoria in New York. In 1983, so the story goes, the editor-in-chief of Bantam Books, who also used this barber, asked him to arrange an introduction to Lee Iacocca. The book developed out of this meeting was *Iacocca,* and it became a breakthrough book with multimillion-copy sales in hardcover, and then a multimillion-copy paperback. (An interesting note is that the barber sued Bantam for an agent's commission. The case was settled out of court.)

The table of contents in *Iacocca* is an excellent model because of its depth and organization. A reader can see the four sections of the book, the chronology of the story, and the author's advice, which concludes the book. The scope, depth, and pace of the book is set forth on this one-page table of contents. It does not get much better, or simpler, than this.

Sample Nonfiction Table of Contents

CONTENTS

Expanded Table of Contents

In some instances, the table of contents for a nonfiction book can be expanded to form a detailed chapter outline. If your subject lends itself to this type of treatment, use this model as an idea generator.

The editor receiving an expanded table of contents can tell by reading a few pages what the book will include, the tone of the book, and the pace, and can anticipate the reader's interest in the subject. She will be impressed by your detailed preparation and thoughtful organization. Many experienced editors find a description of what will appear in each chapter far preferable to a "naked" table of contents.

Following is an example of an expanded table of contents for a nonfiction book, *The Business of Publishing*, created by the author to illustrate this technique.

Sample Nonfiction Expanded Table of Contents

THE BUSINESS OF PUBLISHING

Part I—The Editorial Process

Chapter I. From the Idea to the Creation of the Business
The business of publishing begins with the editorial decision. If it is a start-up business, this is the most crucial of all decisions. What does the author offer the consumer that is unique or, if not unique, published better than ever before? S&S started with a line of crossword puzzle books. Harry Abrams, the distinguished art book publisher, started with a line of books, "The Library of Great Painters." Random House started with Modern Library. Each of these publishing stories will be told dramatically.

Chapter II. How Editorial Decisions Make Businesses Grow
Often, the editorial decisions are more narrowly focused. In some instances, it is a decision as to whether or not to start or add a line (stories of how *The How and Why Books* were started, and how John Muir moved into juvenile publishing when the travel book business was adversely affected by the recession in travel). But still, it is a decision that is made on a title-by-title basis.

Chapter III. The Sources for Books
Where do books come from? From agents, from packagers, from direct solicitation of an author (finding an article in a magazine written by an author you wish to develop), and from the unsolicited manuscript. The most creative form of editorial development is to bring an idea and author together and work to develop both. Or to be able to recognize the talent in an author that can be developed in another genre (Erica Jong from poet to novelist). Or to find a book that, with editing, can be made into a best-seller (story of Don Fine converting *Storm Island* into *Eye of the Needle*). One final, more difficult source, unless you are well qualified, is foreign translation (story of *Arcade*).

Chapter IV. How Editorial Departments Are Organized
Organization chart of the editorial department. The functions to be performed are merged in smaller organizations and done by fewer people (story of a $5 million art book company staffed by three full-time people, with all the rest working on a freelance basis).

Chapter V. The Editorial Process
The process: (1) the book is read by the acquiring editor; (2) there is an informal conference or a short write-up prepared for the editor-in-chief; (3) the editor-in-chief makes the first decision to accept or reject; (4) if the book is deemed to be publishable, it is submitted to the editorial conference, where it may be accepted or rejected; (5) the financial terms are set

by the editor-in-chief and a business manager; (6) the acquiring editor negotiates the terms with the author; (7) the negotiated terms are transmitted to the contract department, where the contract is prepared.

Chapter VI. Making the Editorial Decision

Using financial and market analysis forms, explain how input is collected from marketing, production, and advertising departments, and how proposal is made to the editorial committee. In a smaller firm, these functions are performed by contacting salesmen or key customers, using a printer or production consultant, etc. Explain and illustrate how pricing and format (hardcover vs. softcover) decisions are made.

If the editorial process ends here, prepare for disaster. The most important part of the process is the postmortem. One year after publication, review the economic projections vs. reality. Learn from your successes and from your failures.

Part II—Production

Chapter VII. The Production Process

The editorial department transmits the manuscript to the production department. The first port of call is copyediting (often done outside the company), and then the manuscript goes to the art department for interior design and cover design. (This section will be illustrated to show the copyedited manuscript as well as interior and cover designs, illustrating the pitfalls and the winning techniques.) There will also be a discussion of how the computer has changed these traditional practices.

Chapter VIII. The Printing Process

A short primer on the various forms of printing with both domestic and foreign sources described with tips on when to use a domestic source and when to go abroad.

Part III—Marketing

Chapter IX. Making Marketing Decisions

How the basic marketing decisions are made. How the marketing department is involved in the production and editorial decisions (for instance, pricing, number of pages, title, copy lines, reviewer quotes on the jacket, etc.) when the book is acquired. The "team" approach to publishing.

Chapter X. The Many Markets for Books

Each area of selling the book is examined: independent trade, chain stores, superstores, wholesalers, special sales, foreign sales. Starts with the organization of the marketing department and follows through with who does what and why.

Chapter XI. Book Advertising
The role of advertising as related to the realities of how much a publisher can spend and where to spend it (author tours, print space, radio, TV, etc.). Illustrated with a typical campaign.

Chapter XII. The New Developments in Marketing
The new developments in the mass market, super wholesalers such as Sams, Advanced Marketing, etc. will be discussed along with more traditional areas of the bargain book and remainder markets, book clubs, and direct mail, plus how to use a Web page.

Chapter XIII. Book Fairs
A section on the shows to attend (for example, Frankfurt, BEA, London Book Fair, Bologna, etc.). The value of the fairs and how to get maximum benefit.

Part IV—Financial
Chapter XIV. The Role of the Financial Officer
The role of the financial officer in publishing, illustrating how the finance department is involved in the editorial, production, and marketing decisions. The publishing proposal will be described and illustrated. Illustrations and descriptions of a monthly and annual operating statement, a balance sheet. What smaller publishers need to know if they are to relate to a bank officer in getting and maintaining their line of credit. The fulfillment of orders, described with special emphasis on the customer service aspect of order processing.

Part V—Management
Chapter XV. The Role of the Manager
Primarily written for the manager, demonstrates the varying types of organizational structures to accomplish the mission of the publishing house. Defining the mission, planning, personnel matters, including salary and benefits. A "soft" section on techniques (how to motivate, evaluate, fire people).

Appendix
This will be a current list of reference materials. The text will have endnotes, referring to books, articles, and other materials that would slow up the narrative if included in the body of the book.

Sample Chapter—Fiction

After the editor has been captivated by your cover letter, read the summary and (for nonfiction) the table of contents, she now wishes to see if you *really* can write the book. She turns, excitedly, to the sample chapter. This must close the sale.

The first chapter in a work of fiction must entice the editor to read on. The next chapter will show her that you can build and sustain reader interest. Editors prefer to read one or two chapters in sequence. In rare instances, it might be better to use a pivotal chapter, one which you feel is especially strong. After reading your chapters, she may ask to see the rest of your book, have it receive further consideration, and then, hopefully, recommend that the editorial committee buy the book. But to move in this direction, after reading only a sample chapter, the question that must be answered with a "yes" is, "Would the reader now wish to read the rest of this book and spend several hours with the author?"

To enable you to compare your work with the best, I have enclosed Chapter 1 from *True Grit* by Charles Portis as an example of a chapter of a fictional work that establishes tone and language, introduces language, introduces vivid characters, and makes the reader interested in continuing. Read the first sentence and notice all the information it contains to get the reader off to a fast start. As you probably know, *True Grit* was a major best-seller in hardcover and paperback and later became an excellent film.

The first chapter introduces the narrator and heroine, a fourteen-year-old girl, and sets up the premise of the book, the style, and the pace. The prose is simple, clean, and engaging. An editor reading this would know that she was about to publish a very special book.

True Grit
By Charles Portis

CHAPTER ONE

People do not give it credence that a fourteen-year-old girl could leave home and go off in the wintertime to avenge her father's blood but it did not seem too strange then, although I will say it did not happen every day. I was just fourteen years of age when a coward going by the name of Tom Chaney shot my father down in Fort Smith, Arkansas, and robbed him of his life and his horse and $150 in cash money plus two California gold pieces that he carried in his trouser band.

Here is what happened. We had clear title to 480 acres of good bottom land on the south bank of the Arkansas River not far from Dardanelle in Yell County, Arkansas. Tom Chaney was a tenant but working for hire and not on shares. He turned up one day hungry and riding a gray horse that had a filthy blanket on his back and a rope halter instead of a bridle. Papa took pity on the fellow and gave him a job and a place to live. It was a cotton house made over into a little cabin. It had a good roof.

Tom Chaney said he was from Louisiana. He was a short man with cruel features. I will tell more about his face later. He carried a Henry rifle. He was a bachelor about twenty-five years of age.

In November when the last of the cotton was sold Papa took it in his head to go to Fort Smith and buy some ponies. He had heard that a stock trader there named Colonel Stonehill had bought a large parcel of cow ponies from Texas drovers on their way to Kansas and was now stuck with them. He was getting shed of them at bargain rates as he did not want to feed them over the winter. People in Arkansas did not think much of Texas mustang ponies. They were little and mean. They had never had anything but grass to eat and did not weigh over eight hundred pounds.

Papa had an idea they would make good deer-hunting ponies, being hardy and small and able to keep up with the dogs through the brush. He thought he would buy a small string of them and if things worked out he would breed and sell them for that purpose. His head was full of schemes. Anyway, it would be a cheap enough investment to start with, and we had a patch of winter oats and plenty of hay to see the ponies through till spring when they could graze in our big north pasture and feed on greener and juicier clover than they ever saw in the "Lone Star State." As I recollect, shelled corn was something under fifteen cents a bushel then.

Papa intended for Tom Chaney to stay and look after things on the place while he was gone. But Chaney set up a fuss to go and after a time he got the best of Papa's good nature. If Papa had a failing it was his kindly disposition. People would use him. I did not get my mean streak from him. Frank Ross was the gentlest, most honorable man who ever lived. He had a common-school education. He was a Cumberland Presbyterian and a Mason and he fought with determination at the battle of Elkhorn Tavern but was not wounded in that "scrap" as Lucille Biggers Langford states in her Yell County Yesterdays. I think I am in a position to know the facts. He was hurt in the terrible fight at Chickamauga up in the state of Tennessee and came near to dying on the way home from want of proper care.

Before Papa left for Fort Smith he arranged for a colored man named Yarnell Poindexter to feed the stock and look in on Mama and us every day. Yarnell and his family lived just below us on some land he rented from the bank. He was born of free parents in Illinois but a man named Bloodworth kidnapped him in Missouri and brought him down to Arkansas just before the war. Yarnell was a good man, thrifty and industrious, and he later became a prosperous house painter in Memphis, Tennessee. We exchanged letters every Christmas until he passed away in the flu epidemic of 1918. To this day I have never met anybody else named Yarnell, white or black. I attended the funeral and visited in Memphis with my brother, Little Frank, and his family.

Instead of going to Fort Smith by steamboat or train, Papa decided he would go on horseback and walk the ponies back all tied together. Not only would it be cheaper but it would be a pleasant outing for him and a good ride. Nobody loved to gad about on a prancing steed more than Papa. I have never been very fond of horses myself although I believe I was accounted a good enough rider in my youth. I never was afraid of animals. I remember once I rode a mean goat through a plum thicket on a dare.

From our place to Fort Smith was about seventy miles as a bird flies, taking you past beautiful Mount Nebo where we had a little summer house so Mama could get away from the mosquitos, and also Mount Magazine, the highest point in Arkansas, but it might as well have been seven hundred miles for all I knew of Fort Smith. The boats went up there and some people sold their cotton up there but that was all I knew about it. We sold our cotton down in Little Rock. I had been there two or three times.

Papa left us on his saddle horse, a big chestnut mare with a blazed face called Judy. He took some food and a change of clothes rolled up in some blankets and covered with a slicker. This was tied behind his saddle. He wore his belt gun which was a big long dragoon pistol, the cap-and-ball kind that was old-fashioned even at that time. He had carried it in the war. He was a handsome sight and in my memory's eye I can still see him mounted up there on Judy in his brown woolen coat and black Sunday hat and the both of them, man and beast, blowing little clouds of steam on that frosty morn. He might have been a gallant knight of old. Tom Chaney rode his gray horse that was better suited to pulling a middlebuster than carrying a rider. He had no hand gun but he carried his rifle slung across his back on a piece of cotton plow line. There is trash for you. He could have taken an old piece of harness and made a nice leather strap for it. That would have been too much trouble.

Papa had right around two hundred and fifty dollars in his purse as I had reason to know since I kept his books for him. Mama was never any good at sums and she could hardly spell cat. I do not boast of my own gifts in that direction. Figures and letters are not everything. Like Martha I have always been agitated and troubled by the cares of the day but my mother had a serene and loving heart. She was like Mary and had chosen "that good part." The two gold pieces that Papa carried concealed in his clothes were a marriage gift from my Grandfather Spurling in Monterey, California.

Little did Papa realize that morning that he was never to see us or hold us again, nor would he ever again harken to the meadowlarks of Yell County trilling a joyous anthem to spring.

The news came like a thunderclap. Here is what happened. Papa and Tom Chaney arrived in Fort Smith and took a room at the Monarch boardinghouse. They called on Stonehill at his stock barn and looked over the ponies. It fell out that there was not a mare in the lot, or a stallion for that matter. The Texas cowboys rode nothing but geldings for some cowboy reasons of their own and you can imagine they are no good for breeding purposes. But Papa was not to be turned back. He was determined to own some of those little brutes and on the second day he bought four of them for one hundred dollars even, bringing Stonehill down from his asking price of one hundred and forty dollars. It was a good enough buy.

They made plans to leave the next morning. That night Tom Chaney went to a barroom and got into a game of cards with some "riffraff" like himself and lost his wages. He did not take the loss like a man but went back to the room at the boardinghouse and sullied up like a possum. He had a bottle of whiskey and he drank that. Papa was sitting in the parlor talking to some drummers. By and by Chaney came out of the bedroom with his rifle. He said he had been cheated and was going back to the barroom and get his money. Papa said if he had been cheated then they had best go talk to the law about it. Chaney would not listen. Papa followed him outside and told him to surrender the rifle as he was in no fit state to start a quarrel with a gun in his hand. My father was not armed at the time.

Tom Chaney raised his rifle and shot him in the forehead, killing him instantly. There was no more provocation than that and I tell it as it was told to me by the high sheriff of Sebastian County. Some people might say, well, what business was it of Frank Ross to meddle? My answer is this: he was trying to do that short devil a good turn. Chaney was a tenant and Papa felt responsibility. He was his brother's keeper. Does that answer your question.

Now the drummers did not rush out to grab Chaney or shoot him but instead scattered like poultry while Chaney took my father's purse from his warm body and ripped open the trouser band and took the gold pieces too. I cannot say how he knew about them. When he finished his thieving he raced to the end of the street and struck the night watchman at the stock barn a fierce blow to the mouth with his rifle stock, knocking him silly. He put a bridle on Papa's horse Judy and rode out bareback. Darkness swallowed him up. He might have taken the time to saddle the horse or hitched up three spans of mules to a Concord stagecoach and smoked a pipe as it seems no one in that city was after him. He had mistaken the drummers for men. "The wicked flee when none pursueth."

Sample Chapter—Nonfiction

A useful nonfiction sample comprises the first two chapters of *Where Angels Walk* by Joan Wester Anderson and published by Barton & Brett Publishers, Inc. This book was produced after editorial discussions between the author and her future publishers, who believed in its potential strongly enough to start their own company to publish it. As its best-seller status and subsequent sales demonstrated, it was indeed an excellent subject for a book. It helped usher in a boom in angel books over the next few years.

This model demonstrates the need for more than one chapter. Had Joan Wester Anderson initially submitted a cover letter, a summary, and a table of contents to an unknown publisher, the editor reviewing it might wonder how the author would handle the subject and sustain interest. Chapters 1 and 2, taken together, show her abilities amply. The opening anecdote demonstrates the author's ability to tell a story, her use of dialogue, imagery, language, and finally her ability to surprise the reader. The second chapter illustrates the thrust of the book.

Where Angels Walk
By Joan Wester Anderson

THE BEGINNING . . .

A guardian angel o'er his life presiding,
Doubling his pleasures, and his cares dividing.
Samuel Rogers, *Human Life*

It was just past midnight on December 24, 1983. The Midwest was shivering through a record-breaking cold spell, complete with gale force winds and frozen water pipes. And although our suburban Chicago household was filled with the snug sounds of a family at rest, I couldn't be a part of them, not until our twenty-one-year-old son pulled into the driveway. At the moment, Tim and his two roommates were driving home for Christmas, their first trip back since they had moved East last May. "Don't worry, Mom," Tim had reassured me over the phone last night. "We're going to leave before dawn tomorrow and drive straight through. We'll be fine."

Kids. They do insane things. Under normal circumstances, I figured a Connecticut-to-Illinois trek ought to take about eighteen hours. But the weather had turned so dangerously cold that radio reports warned against venturing outdoors, even for a few moments. And we had heard nothing from the travelers. Distressed, I pictured them on a desolate road. What if they ran into car problems or lost their way? And if they had been delayed, why hadn't Tim phoned? Restlessly I paced and prayed in the familiar shorthand all mothers know: God, send someone to help them.

By now, as I later learned, the trio had stopped briefly in Fort Wayne, Indiana, to deposit Don at his family home. Common sense suggested that Tim and Jim stay the rest of the night and resume their trek in the morning. But when does common sense prevail with invincible young adults? There were only four driving hours left to reach home. And although it was the coldest night in Midwest history and the highways were snowy and deserted, the two had started out again.

They had been traveling for only a few miles on a rural access road to the Indiana tollway, when they noticed that the car's engine seemed sluggish, lurching erratically and dying to ten or fifteen miles per hour. Tim glanced uneasily at Jim. "Do not—" the radio announcer intoned, "—repeat—do not venture outside tonight, friends. There's a record windchill of eighty below zero, which means that exposed skin will freeze in less than a minute." The car surged suddenly, then coughed and slowed again.

"Tim," Jim spoke into the darkness, "we're not going to stall here, are we?"

"We can't," Tim answered grimly as he pumped the accelerator. "We'd die for sure."

But instead of picking up speed, the engine sputtered, chugging and slowing again. About a mile later, at the top of a small incline, the car crawled to a frozen stop.

Horrified, Tim and Jim looked at each other in the darkened interior. They could see across the fields in every direction, but, incredibly, theirs was the only vehicle in view. For the first time, they faced the fact that they were in enormous danger. There was no traffic, no refuge ahead, not even a farmhouse light blinking in the distance. It was as if they had landed on an alien, snow-covered planet.

And the appalling, unbelievable cold! Never in Tim's life had he experienced anything so intense. They couldn't run for help; he knew that now for sure. He and Jim were young and strong, but even if shelter was only a short distance away, they couldn't survive. The temperature would kill them in a matter of minutes.

"Someone will come along soon," Jim muttered, looking in every direction. "They're bound to."

"I don't think so," Tim said. "You heard the radio. Everyone in the world is inside tonight—except us."

"Then what are we going to do?"

"I don't know." Tim tried starting the engine again, but the ignition key clicked hopelessly in the silence. Bone-chilling cold had penetrated the car's interior, and his feet were already growing numb. Well, God, he prayed, echoing my own distant plea, You're the only one who can help us now.

It seemed impossible to stay awake much longer. . . . Then, as if they had already slipped into a dream, they saw headlights flashing at the car's left rear. But that was impossible. For they had seen no twin pinpricks of light in the distance, no hopeful approach. Where had the vehicle come from? Had they already died?

But no. For, miraculously, someone was knocking on the driver's side window. "Need to be pulled?" In disbelief they heard the muffled shout. But it was true. Their rescuer was driving a tow truck.

"Yes! Oh, yes, thanks!" Quickly, the two conferred as the driver, saying nothing more, drove around to the front of the car and attached chains. If there were no garages open at this hour, they would ask them to take them back to Don's house, where they could spend the rest of the night.

Swathed almost completely in a furry parka, hood and a scarf up to his eyes, the driver nodded at their request but said nothing more. He was calm, they noted as he climbed into his truck, seeming unconcerned about the life-threatening circumstances in which he had found them. Strange that he's not curious about us, Tim mused, and he isn't even explaining where he came from or how he managed to approach without our seeing him. . . . And had there been lettering on the side of the truck? Tim hadn't noticed any. He's going to give us a big bill, on a night like this. I'll have to borrow some money from Don or his dad. . . . But Tim was exhausted from the ordeal, and gradually, as he leaned against the seat, his thoughts slipped away.

They passed two locked service stations, stopped to alert Don from a pay phone, and were soon being towed back through the familiar Fort Wayne neighborhood. Hushed, Christmas lights long since extinguished and families asleep, Don's still seemed the most welcoming street they had ever been on. The driver maneuvered carefully around the cul-de-sac and pulled up in front of Don's house. Numb with cold, Tim and Jim raced to the side door where Don was waiting, then tumbled into the blessedly warm kitchen, safe at last.

Don slammed the door against the icy blast. "Hey, what happened?" he began, but Tim interrupted.

"The tow-truck driver, Don—I have to pay him. I need to borrow—"

"Wait a minute." Don frowned, looking past his friends through the window. "I don't see any tow truck out there."

Tim and Jim turned around. There, parked alone at the curb, was Tim's car. There had been no sound in the crystal-clear night of its release from the chains, no door slam, no chug of an engine pulling away. There had been no bill for Tim to pay, no receipt to sign, no farewell or "thank you" or "Merry Christmas. . . ." Stunned, Tim raced back down the driveway to the curb, but there were no taillights disappearing in the distance, no engine noise echoing through the silent streets, nothing at all to mark the tow truck's presence.

Then Tim saw the tire tracks traced in the windblown snowdrifts. But there was only one set of marks ringing the cul-de-sac curve. And they belonged to Tim's car. . . .

When Christmas carols fill the air and our worries regress in a temporary whirl of holiday nostalgia, everyone believes in angels. But it's harder to accept the likelihood that the "multitude of heavenly host" on that long-ago Bethlehem hillside has relevance in our lives too, that God's promise to send His angels to protect and rescue each of His children is a faithful pact, continuing for all eternity, throughout every season of the year.

Angels don't get much attention today. If the spirit world is acknowledged at all, it's usually the dark side, the bizarre satanic cults that are wreaking so much havoc, especially among our youth. Yet there is evidence that good spirits are also at work here on earth—combating evil, bringing news, warning us of danger, consoling us in our suffering . . . then vanishing, just as the angels did on that first Christmas night.

Angels don't submit to litmus tests, testify in court, or slide under a microscope for examination. Thus, their existence cannot be "proved" by the guidelines we humans usually use. To know one, perhaps, requires a willingness to suspend judgment, to open ourselves to possibilities we've only dreamed about. "The best and most beautiful things in the world cannot be seen or even touched," Helen Keller said. "They must be felt with the heart."

Was it an angel? Our family will never know for sure.

But on Christmas Eve in 1983, I heard the whisper of wings as a tow-truck driver answered a heavenly summons and brought our son safely home.

SEARCHING FOR ANSWERS

We not only live among men, but there are
airy hosts, blessed spectators, sympathetic
lookers-on, that see and know and appreciate
our thoughts and feelings and acts.
                    Henry Ward Beecher, *Royal Truths*

Angels. What did I really know about these celestial beings? As a Catholic, I was certainly aware of their existence. During childhood, I had learned a prayer to my guardian angel, and in college I had studied the hierarchy of angels, the nine choirs, each with its own function and assignment. But after Tim's curious rescue, I began to research angels with deeper interest.

One of the first facts I uncovered was a Gallup poll suggesting that more than sixty percent of Americans believe wholeheartedly in angels. Although scholars differ about specifics, their existence is accepted by all three of the great Western religions—Judaism, Christianity, and Islam. Angels are mentioned more than three hundred times in Sacred Scripture, acting alone or in great gatherings, carrying out God's commands, forming a heavenly court, and—significantly—protecting and bringing messages to people. They played crucial roles in the Old Testament, including the books of the Jewish Torah, and are cited frequently in the Islamic Koran. Socrates often asked his guardian angel for advice. Many famous saints, as well as Salvation Army founder General William Booth, claimed to have seen angels, and Abraham Lincoln said he felt their presence frequently. Celestial beings appear in the works of Dante, Milton, and Shakespeare, as well as in the works of contemporary authors.

As civilization evolved, so did humanity's understanding of angels. To early pagans, gods seemed either to be stars and planets or to dwell in the sky, so it was a simple transition to consider angels as winged spirits who could travel easily between heaven and earth.

Interpretations varied as time passed. Early Hebrews contended that the universe was a hierarchy, with God at the top and other entities radiating downward from Him. They believed that angels constitute the "court of heaven." In writings they referred to "the angels of God," and bene Elohim, "God's sons."

Christians believe that God made angels at or about the time He made the world (Saint Augustine thought the two acts of creation were simultaneous), but before He created human beings. They were given minds and wills, like us, but had no bodies. At some point, according to the Book of Revelation, some of the angels wished to be gods and there was a terrible battle in heaven. The defeated angels then became evil spirits, headed by

Satan, who roam the world to this day. The Council of Nicaea in 325 declared belief in angels a dogma, but a later synod condemned the worship of angels.

Muslims also believe that angels were created before man. According to the Koran, when humans were fashioned God's supreme handiwork, angels were required to bow down before them, an order that prompted Lucifer's rebellion. Before Muhammad united them under one religious banner of Islam, the Arabs had recognized many gods and goddesses and had seemed to include angels among them. Muhammad acknowledged Biblical writings, and thus included angels in his new religion. In fact, after being chosen as Prophet, Muhammad claimed to see a beautiful vision of Gabriel, who promised to guide him in his new role. Muslims believe that angels witness for or against people on the Day of Judgment, and that recording angels are present at prayer in the mosque and elsewhere.

My investigations revealed that, whatever their beginnings, angels have three basic purposes: to worship God, to serve as heralds between God and His people on earth, and to act as our caretakers, while never interfering with our free will. Saint Dionysius, Saint Paul, Pope Gregory, and others further divide angels into nine choirs, listed here in descending order, along with their main duties: Seraphim and Cherubim, who love and worship God; Thrones and Dominions, who regulate angelic duties; Virtues, who work miracles on earth; Powers, who protect us from demons; Principalities, Archangels, and Angels, who are ministers and guardians of people.

The four archangels best known to us are Raphael, Michael, Gabriel, and Uriel. Their numbers seem to be infinite, though, and throughout history, others have also been named. One of the oldest shrines in Turkey is dedicated to Michael, who is considered a great healer of the sick in that nation. Although angels are extremely powerful, they are, of course, subject to God in all things.

Religions differ on specifics about angels: for example, most Catholics believe that everyone receives a guardian angel at birth, a life companion especially suited to one's unique personality. Catholic children learn a comforting little prayer to initiate "conversation" with their angel, and the feast day of guardian angels is celebrated on October second. Ancient Jewish angelology also taught the personal-angel theory. In fact, the Talmud speaks of every Jew being assigned eleven thousand guardian angels at birth! The various Protestant faiths hold divergent views, most believing that we shouldn't pray to angels, but that we may ask them to intervene for us.

As angels began to appear in art, around the fourth century, artists gave them wings in order to distinguish them from the apostles or other holy men and women. We also think of them as dimpled cherubs, or perhaps a white-garbed chorus, as on that first Christmas night. Survivors of near-death experiences, however, cite "bright beings of light" that they met along the way—a reminder that light, symbolized in artists' renditions by halos or luminous bodies, represents heaven and, perhaps, those occupying it.

In Scripture, many angels appear as powerful, fearless soldiers. But there are also Bible stories about men and women meeting angels in human form, angels who look just like ordinary mortals . . . actually, just like Tim's angel. The companion in the Book of Tobit and the strangers who visit Lot in Genesis are good examples. And did not Saint Paul admonish the Hebrews—and all who would come after them—to "show hospitality, for by that means some have entertained angels without knowing it"?

The more I read, the more I realized that far from being outdated, angels are part of today's world too. There are cities, sports teams, aviator groups, and charitable activities named after angels. Members of the national street safety patrol known as the Guardian Angels wear T-shirts with an emblem featuring an eye, wings, and a shield denoting, according to founder and director Curtis Sliwa, "angellike protection offered to everyone, even those who don't want us looking out for them." There is an Angel Collectors Club of America, a national association of angel lovers with its own newsletter and annual convention. Angel Threads, a children's boutique, operates in Tucson. There is an Angels in Heaven day nursery in Cleveland and an angel collectible mail-order business in Riverside, California. Toller Cranston lives in a Toronto house filled with angel paintings, mobiles, and other celestial art; this six-time Canadian figure-skating champion likes angels because, he says, "they can leave gravity behind."

Even Hollywood gets into the angel act on occasion. Who can forget Clarence in the movie "It's a Wonderful Life," a lovable, bumbling angel who shows a suicidal man (James Stewart) the value of his life and what would have happened if he had not been true to his principles? Stewart has always maintained that the role was his favorite. "Field of Dreams," while not specifically about angel spirits, made such an impact on moviegoers that the baseball field in Iowa where it was filmed still attracts thousands of tourists every year.

And consider the popular television series "Highway to Heaven," produced by the late Michael Landon. Landon played the role of an angel, Jonathan Smith, sent from heaven to persuade hurting people to help one another. The idea had come to Landon one day while, stuck in traffic on a Los Angeles freeway, he watched drivers angrily honk and yell at one another. If they used even a fraction of that energy on being kind, Landon mused, how the world could be changed! Soon he developed a series based on the idea that kindness, not anger, solves problems, with the central character an angel who could make mistakes but could also be a spiritual catalyst in people's lives.

But Hollywood is fiction. Were real angels still around today, still ministering to us by caress, whisper—or in human form? If this dramatic, unexpected, and marvelously loving rescue had happened to my son, would I find that others had similar stories? It seemed logical; since I believe God loves all His children with equal intensity, He would certainly tender to everyone the same protection he had provided to Tim. But maybe few of us recognized this help when it came. Or perhaps we passed such moments off as "lucky breaks" or "coincidence." I would have to dig deeper to find the answers.

But it was one thing to read privately about angels, quite another to ask someone, even a close friend, "Have you ever met an angel?" People vary in their willingness to trust the supernatural, I think. Many consider the idea of heavenly beings walking around helping humans as incomprehensible. We are, after all, creatures of the twentieth century's "theology" of scientific proof. Others agree that such an encounter might occur, that we live in a world where not everything is explainable in logical terms, but they maintain that real miracles wouldn't—couldn't—happen to them. After all, didn't one have to be exceptionally pious in order to qualify? And if I found people who had an encounter similar to Tim's, would they be willing to share it?

Taking a deep breath, I went to the post office and rented a box. Then I wrote to magazines where readers were familiar with my byline and asked that my letter be published: I am looking for people who believe they may have met an angel, I wrote. I am not talking about human beings who, because of kindly deeds, might rightfully be called "angels." I am talking about spirits who appeared in human form to give some kind of help. Please write to me at this box number. . . .

A few of the magazine editors wrote back stating that they didn't publish letters of this kind. They either objected to having their pages used as a means of research or, I suspect, considered my request a bit too weird. From others, I received no acknowledgment. This could mean a decision to discard my letter—or publish it. But even if my request was honored, what if no one responded? What if readers laughed or, worse, said to one another, "That Joan Anderson used to be a nice, normal writer. But I think she's gone round the bend, don't you?"

I waited, kept looking for angel material, and, one day, saw one of my requests in print. A few weeks later I went to the post office, inserted my key into my rented box and gathered my courage. This was probably what people called "the moment of truth." Today I would discover whether Tim's event was an isolated occurrence—or whether we were members of a great and glorious community of people whose lives had been touched by a heavenly being.

I swung open the mailbox door—and stepped back in amazement. It was filled with envelopes.

The Bio

The author with extensive credits, especially of previously published articles or books, does not have a problem in establishing her credibility, especially when submitting an excellent book proposal. But the author with limited background must include as much as she can to illustrate her qualifications (though a bio should never be more than a page). Following are two samples of a bio—one in résumé form and one in narrative form.

The sample résumé bio provides the author's salient information: address, phone, fax at home and at work, the college education, which in this case is in English Literature and Education, and her present teaching career (this is designed to give the editor confidence in the author's ability to write at an acceptable level). The fact that the author, Mary Carol Smith, has written published articles provides additional assurance that her writing could be commercially acceptable. Note especially that Mary Carol Smith includes her public appearances on television and radio as evidence that she would feel comfortable promoting her own book if required. The author who can effectively promote her own book on radio and television has a special skill that may tip the scales in her favor. When the editor looks at the entire proposal, likes what she has read, and reads this bio, she should be reassured and ready to consider the proposal favorably.

Some editors prefer to see a narrative bio much like the second sample as another measure of the author's ability to write effectively. Make your bio the best you can and tailor it as much as you can to your book's subject. Bios are as different as the people they reflect. Remember, even if you do not have a long list of credentials, many who were self-taught, such as Abraham Lincoln, were also best-selling and long-lasting authors. He even became president of the United States.

Sample Résumé Bio

Mary Carol Smith

Home:
1234 South 21st Street
Philadelphia, PA 19765

Office:
Department of English
New Smyrna Junior College
Box 1234
New Smyrna, DE 65431

Home Telephone:
215-555-5674
Fax: 215-555-5675

Office Telephone:
307-555-6339
Fax: 307-555-9396

Birthdate: July 4, 1952

Education:
North Carolina State University, Chapel Hill, NC
B.S. in Education, June 1974
M.A. in English Literature, June 1976
Additional Writing Courses, Tanglewood, MA, Summer 1990, 1992
Career Highlights:
Associate Professor, English
New Smyrna Junior College, 1986–present
Teach Freshman English and Creative Writing

Previous Publications:
Have written over 1,000 articles, some of which have been published nationally in *Ladies' Home Journal, Family Circle, Modern Bride, Christian Science Monitor,* and *American Baby.* One article, "My Husband the Baby," appeared in *Reader's Digest.* While raising my two children, now almost adults, I wrote at home with reasonable success.

Public Appearances:
While in college I was a model, selected by Breck Shampoo for its national advertising.
As member of the Executive Committee of Planned Parenthood and in charge of the Outreach Program, I make speeches and appear on television and radio.

The Book Proposal:
Pulling It All Together

From what you have read you can assemble a proposal incorporating the segments described and illustrated on pages 52–54. Your proposal should contain:

- a cover letter
- a summary
- a table of contents (most important for nonfiction)
- a sample chapter
- a bio

In all, the author would send twelve to twenty-four pages to the publisher—certainly not a complete manuscript. The editors I interviewed agree—the shorter the presentation, the more likely it will be read.

In the following pages there are two model proposals. The first is for *Don Juan de Marco*, a movie tie-in novel published by Penguin Books.* The second proposal is for a nonfiction book, a hostel-goers guide called *Bed Ahead*, which was prepared by two readers of the first edition of this book, Evan Halper and Paul Karr, and resulted in the book being acquired and published by Globe Pequot Press, a leading travel publisher.

---

*This model proposal was based upon the book *Don Juan de Marco*, a novel written by Jean Blake White based upon a screenplay by Jeremy Leven. The summary was written by the author of this book. The table of contents, the prologue, and the chapter were written by Jean Blake White and are reprinted by her courtesy. *Don Juan de Marco* was released by New Line Cinemas as a major motion picture featuring Marlon Brando, Johnny Depp, and Faye Dunaway.

Proposal 1—Don Juan de Marco

The subject of this proposal is an exotic work of fiction concerning a man who believes he is Don Juan. The purpose of this sample is to demonstrate that a proposal even for a major work can be effectively presented in a modest number of typewritten, double-spaced pages (single-spaced here to save space), and to encourage you to use this well-tested, successful method that is likely to attract an editor's attention and a positive response. The summary and the table of contents position the chapter.

The Cover Letter

October 26, 1994

Ms. Mary K. Wright
Doublemint Publishing
1234 Wrigley Blvd.
Chicago, IL 23456

Dear Mary K. Wright:

Byron, Shaw, Rostand, and Corneille wrote about him; Gluck, Mozart, and Strauss placed this legendary lover in music. And now, he appears in a modern contemporary novel, reinterpreted for today's audience. None other than Don Juan.

I found Byron's unfinished epic poem *Don Juan* so filled with love and joy that I have written a novel which will run about 100,000 words, *Don Juan de Marco,* which puts Don Juan in the center of our culture.

Read how Johnny de Marco, aka Don Juan, goes from the cape, the Spanish hat with the tassel, the brocaded pants, the shiny boots, and the mask to dungarees and then back in costume to find his long-lost love, Donna Anna.

Please read the story synopsis, the table of contents, and a sample of my writing. Please feel free to call me at 212-555-6789 or use the enclosed self-addressed, stamped envelope to reply.

Sincerely,

Karl K. Klopfer

The Summary of the Novel

Summary

The story opens with Don Juan de Marco entering his favorite restaurant. He is dressed in a cape, black silk pants, a brocaded vest, a Spanish hat with tassels on the brim, and shiny black boots. Of all the women there, he selects Victoria, a beautiful young lady, waiting for her male companion to join her for dinner. Don Juan sends her a bottle of champagne, whisks her away to his bedroom, makes passionate love to her, and returns her to the restaurant just before her escort arrives. We learn Don Juan is the greatest lover known, adored and blessed by the many women he allows to be with him.

The story shifts to downtown Los Angeles, where a man dressed as Don Juan sits beneath a billboard of a semi-nude woman in a bikini advertising a Mexican resort, high above the street. The man is about to jump to his death. The police circle the area and send for the psychiatrist on duty, Dr. Jack Mickler, who arrives and is lifted in a cherry picker to try to talk "Don Juan" down to the street.

Mickler is about to retire, an old hand at suicides, and pretends to be Don Octavio del Flores, an acquaintance of Don Juan, and establishes rapport. "Don Juan" explains he has conquered all the women in the world except the most beautiful, Donna Anna, who is pictured on the billboard, and knowing he can never have her, he must die. Mickler convinces "Don Juan" that he may yet have Donna Anna, who indeed may be longing for him. "Don Juan" is taken by this logic and agrees to come down to the street in the cherry picker with Dr. Mickler, who then accompanies him to the psychiatric hospital at which Mickler practices.

Mickler is a successful psychiatrist married to a younger wife, Marilyn, of about fifty, who is finding life at the menopause period disturbing and loveless. They live together comfortably but not passionately. Mickler is now only ten days from retirement after thirty-five years as the top clinician at the hospital. He finds "Don Juan" fascinating and asks for the opportunity to evaluate "Don Juan" as a patient. Under the law, the hospital has ten days to either commit a patient to an institution or release him.

At first, Mickler's fellow therapists resist but when "Don Juan" himself says he will only speak to Don Octavio del Flores, the character Mickler assumed when he talked "Don Juan" down and prevented his jumping, the director of the hospital agrees to give Mickler the ten days to treat "Don Juan," whom they regard as a delusional patient.

In the first session, Mickler attempts to give "Don Juan" medication to combat what he believes are "Don Juan's" delusions. "Don Juan" challenges Mickler to listen to his story before he prescribes the medicine. "Give me ten days," says "Don Juan," "and if I do not convince you that I am really Don Juan, I will take the medicine." And with this, "Don Juan" sets up ten chess pieces, and says, "Each day we will move one piece to mark the time." Mickler agrees.

"Don Juan" begins to tell his story in the first session of therapy. As he tells the story, he says he noticed as a baby when he saw his mother, the beautiful Donna Inez, naked that there was something special about him. Then he found as he grew, girls danced attendance upon him. At ten years of age, he was brought into the church and the priests asked God to save the young Don Juan before it was too late. Apparently God did not hear the plea because Don Juan continued into his puberty to understand the beauty and sexual nature of women and that they desired him passionately, and he had a limitless appetite and ability to satisfy.

Dr. Mickler listens to what he believes are fantasies, and asks "Don Juan" about his real parents. Not pleased, "Don Juan" admits his father was Italian, Tony de Marco, the Dance King of Astoria, and his mother, Donna Inez, was Mexican, the only daughter of a wealthy landowner, who died along with Donna's mother when Donna was young. Donna took over the operation of the plantation and prospered. Tony de Marco, who worked for a pharmaceutical company, was transferred from Queens, New York to Mexico. Tony and Donna met, fell in love, and were married. Tony took over the plantation and became "el patron." Don Juan was born exactly nine months after Tony met Donna Inez. The first session of therapy is over and Mickler is confused, even more so when he finds that the entire female nursing staff looks with great affection on "Don Juan," as he returns to the ward.

In the next session, "Don Juan" describes his first love in poetic detail, ending with a statement to Mickler. "Don Juan" says, "There are only four questions of value in life. What is sacred? Of what is the spirit made? What is worth living for? And dying for?" And the answer, "Don Juan" says, "The answer to each is the same, Don Octavio. It is love." The talk of love is having its effect on Dr. Mickler, who at home meets sexual indifference. The grief in their marriage of many years has taken its toll despite the present aura that "Don Juan" has created.

The sessions continue and "Don Juan" tells the story of how he killed the man who killed his father in a duel and was so ashamed of his role that he forever wore a mask to hide his shame.

To check the reality of the story, Dr. Mickler visits "Don Juan's" grandmother with whom he lived. He is shown to Johnny de Marco's ("Don

Juan's") room, which is covered with magazine photographs of mostly nude girls. Catherine, de Marco's grandmother, tells Mickler that her son, Tony de Marco, Johnny's father, is dead, killed in a car crash in Phoenix. He had never lived in Mexico, and she did not know the location of Johnny's mother.

Mickler confronts "Don Juan" in the next session. He says his grand-mother is delusional, not he. When Mickler confronts him with a photo for the model Chelsea Stoker, whose picture he found on the wall in Johnny's room, "Don Juan" denies this and insists that the photograph is of Donna Anna, whom he loves deeply and has lost forever. Mickler tells him that it is not uncommon for men to fall in love with a photograph of a desirable model, seek to meet her, and failing this, to try to commit suicide. "Don Juan" accuses Dr. Mickler of seeking the easy solution to the therapy because his colleagues would think him delusional if he said he believed the story, accepted him as Don Juan, and discharged him as a rational person. "Don Juan" says he will prove that the picture is really Donna Anna.

At the next therapy session, "Don Juan" tells an exotic story of a trip, his time in a harem, and his being with 1,500 women. The story is told in vivid detail well beyond the bounds of a normal imagination, but he stops short of telling about Donna Anna, which he says is for a later session. What these exotic and sensuous sessions have done is to bring Dr. Mickler, Jack, to realize that he loves his wife and seek her out for sex. He rediscovers his love and his ability to relate to her as a sex partner.

As the sessions continue, the ten days are almost up and the staff has decided, with Dr. Mickler's reluctant agreement, that "Don Juan" should be medicated to remove the delusions. At the beginning of a session, Donna Inez materializes in the room. "Don Juan's" mother testifies to the accuracy of all "Don Juan" has said. Donna Inez tells about the struggle in which Don Juan kills Don Alonzo to avenge his father's death, and therefore must wear the mask to hide his shame. Dr. Mickler challenges "Don Juan" by saying that it appears that in this retelling by Donna Inez, Don Alonzo was the lover of his mother. "Don Juan" is troubled, but the matter rests.

Finally, "Don Juan" tells the story of Donna Anna to Dr. Mickler. Don Juan is shipwrecked and cast upon the sea. Don Juan comes to an island. He finds himself on the beach. He is ministered to by this magnificent crea-ture, Donna Anna. They fall in love. Don Juan finally is ready to plight his troth to this one person. She loves him, too. Before they can get married, Donna Anna says she must hear the story of the mask. Reluctantly Don Juan tells her the story. She then asks how many women Don Juan has made love to. She urges him to be truthful. He tells her the truth, over 1,500. Donna Anna is enraged. She tells him that she, too, has had many lovers, is not what she seems, lashes out at him and runs away . . . forever. His one true love is gone. "Don Juan" asks Dr. Mickler if he believes that he is really Don Juan now that he has heard the story.

Dr. Mickler says he really does believe the story, and shows his agreement by saying he is really Don Octavio del Flores, wed to the great and gentle beauty, Donna Lucita. "Don Juan" takes off his mask and hugs the doctor. Since he is believed, "Don Juan" is then willing to take the medication to remove the delusions. Dr. Mickler says he will return in two days to say good-bye on his last day in the hospital.

Dr. Mickler goes home and convinces his wife, Marilyn, whom he tenderly calls Donna Lucita, that they must liquidate all they own. He returns to the hospital where the medicated "Don Juan" is now dressed in blue jeans and is walking around in a daze. "Don Juan" is then brought to a commitment hearing, required by law before he can be committed. "Don Juan" tells the judge that he is really Johnny de Marco, grew up in Phoenix, fell in love with the centerfold, tried to kill himself, but now realizes that this was an irrational thing to do. The judge says it sounds as though Johnny is cured of his delusion, and discharges him.

When Dr. Mickler returns for the farewell to Johnny, he finds him dressed in blue jeans, ready to go home. He puts Johnny into his car, takes out a bag with his cape and other clothing and gives it to Johnny. They drive to Dr. Mickler's home. At his house, movers are cleaning out all its contents. Jack, his wife, and Johnny drive away to the airport, where they board a plane which takes them to an island that is the island "Don Juan" described in his therapy. When they arrive at the island, Johnny dresses in his Don Juan clothes. Dr. Mickler and Marilyn bring him to the beach and Johnny runs off into the distance, as Marilyn turns to Dr. Mickler and says, "Are you absolutely sure about this, Jack?" They watch as "Don Juan" and Donna Anna embrace.

The Table of Contents

Contents

Sample of Writing

Don Juan de Marco

PROLOGUE: THE LEGEND

The origin of the Don Juan legend is obscure, but its essentials have been cherished for centuries. Don Juan himself was supposed to be Spanish, Italian, or Portuguese. His legend, however, was elaborated by the English, a colder nation but one passionately desirous of warmth. After all, Queen Victoria's empire eventually included a great many palm trees, idyllic islands, and warm-water harbors.

England also produced the works of the warm-blooded romantic and charmingly susceptible George Gordon, Lord Byron, who was given to romantic adventures of various kinds, beginning at a very early age. He loved Greek islands—and a large number of women. He was the author of *Don Juan,* a long and skillful retelling of the legend in verse, satirical but sweet. Some Englishmen, even today, have memorized large swatches of the poem and will whisper it to an appreciative young woman if the setting is just right and the mood sufficiently intoxicating.

The other man who kept the Don Juan legend alive was Wolfgang Amadeus Mozart, the composer of the opera *Don Giovanni,* in which the wicked but adorable Don Juan is consumed by the flames of Hell, defiant to the last. Few men can hum the great themes of this opera, but no one who has ever seen it can forget Don Juan's final repudiation of responsibility and repentance.

In both tellings of the legend, women in great numbers find the don utterly irresistible. His charm is overpowering, his attractions without equal. He never intends to harm anyone, and, though he keeps track of his totals, is not so much interested in scores as in playing well. He never thinks of himself as aggressive but as agreeable.

Don Juan never grew old, having been consumed by infernal flames long before wrinkles and gray hair could set in. In the legend, he remains forever boyish. Neither Don Juan's composer nor his poet ever reached, or perhaps wished to reach, middle age. Mozart died at the age of thirty-five. Byron died in Greece at thirty-six. Both fortunately expired before the prudish realm of Queen Victoria ever got underway.

We all recognize the legend's devotee when we meet him at a party or in a conference room, or even in advertisements in the personals sections of newspapers, though these days he is seldom equipped with a mask or sword or cape; he may even be detected masquerading in a thoroughly unboyish but enthusiastic body. He is often charming but growing cagier every day as women become more prone to laughter. His yearnings are quaint and his intense attachment to the past is rather touching. We must treat him tenderly, knowing so well that he's an antique. Like baseball cards or the Book of Kells, he is to be preserved and lovingly appreciated but never to be played with again. However, Don Juan and his heirs do not, necessarily, yield gracefully to life on the shelf.

And thereby hangs our tale.

CHAPTER 1: DON JUAN AT HOME
In which Don Juan prepares for death.

Slender, young, and languid, Don Juan de Marco reclined alone in a bedroom clearly designed for seduction. His pajamas were silk, and his mask was new. He lay on red satin sheets, reflected in many mirrors. A small fire blazed in the marble fireplace, in front of which a magnificent wolfskin covered the hand-knotted Turkish carpet.

A leather notebook, a slim journal without a title, rested on Don Juan's knees. He was writing his suicide note. Sad songs played on his stereo, which would normally have been pouring out mariachi music, tangos, sambas, or seductive arias from Italian operas.

He had started writing his suicide note more than a month ago. Although his life was short, it had been eventful. He wished to do it justice in his swan song, and justice meant the inclusion of many luscious women and exotic lands, discoveries and losses, and tales of narrow escapes.

He had finally reached the point where it became necessary to explain his reasons for wishing to die. He took up his richly engraved gold pen and began to write.

> I wish to end my life because of a broken heart. The woman responsible for this wish is Donna Anna, my glorious but lost soulmate. A world in which I must live without my darling Donna Anna is one in which I no longer wish to linger, even though I am still the world's greatest lover. I have made love to over a thousand women, a remarkable record for a man of my admittedly tender years.

The thought of the thousand beautiful women made him pause briefly. A tender smile played over his handsome features. His mouth was soft, formed like a cupid's bow. His cheeks were smooth, but since he had achieved his majority, he wore a modest beard and a dashing mustache. His hair was long and curled charmingly over his shoulders. He tapped the pen against his curved lips, a smile of rueful nostalgia continuing to flicker as he considered how best to state his story.

He began to write in a well-formed, calligraphic hand. He made no corrections and the words seemed to flow from his pen without effort.

Like music, gymnastics, or figure skating, the game of love occasionally produces a prodigy, blooming early and fiercely. I am such a prodigy. Zeus himself might have surpassed me in variety of species sampled, but never in zeal. No woman has ever left my arms unsatisfied, but that is of no great consequence now that I have lost the only woman who has ever mattered to me.

He arose from the tumbled sheets and put on a quilted dressing gown with a velvet collar, feeling that his sentiments required more formal garb than pajamas. Then he resumed his writing, a solemn expression on his gentle face, as he contemplated the end of his delightful stay on earth.

Thus, at the prime of my life, and the age of twenty-one, I have determined to end my life this very night.

He paused to consider the best way to proceed. He realized that the name and beauty of his beloved might not be known to the stranger who would read his note. Yet some understanding of his staggering loss was necessary if the situation were to be properly appreciated by that stranger.

The incomparable Donna Anna was once all my own, then was lost to me forever. I was shipwrecked, washed up on the shore like a bit of seaweed, found by a beautiful girl and cast again into the deep. Blighted affections, that's my problem. But as you read my story, stranger, think of a blazing beach, coffee and ouzo, and the burnished shoulders of a silk-draped, cherry-lipped virgin warbling innocently beside the amniotic waters of the Aegean.

You will say, of course, that after all, I had her. We grappled naked as the cruise boats sailed past. A hoopoe perched on the columns of the ruined temple, watching our acrobatic couplings with avian amazement. You will be puzzled by my determination to die, considering the net of lust we crocheted around our laboring bodies, the giving and taking and tasting and rolling over and over, shameless, and both as beautiful as sunfish. I surely had her, you will think, this boy enjoyed the fondest liberties, the most intimate secrets of his darling, and he possessed her completely.

Don Juan stopped to mop his brow. The room had grown much warmer. He shed his dressing gown and began to write the end of his note.

You would be wrong, you who judge me foolish, because for once and forever, she possessed me. There on the magic island, in the cool sea air scented with honeysuckle and thyme, in the shade of olives, on the picnic table, she took what once was my heart and she threw it away.

Lewdness is no substitute for love. My genius was that I never gave less than both to any woman. Round or thin, blond, brunette or blue-haired, I drew out the best in every one of them, until an accident of navigation cast me up on that infernal beach, on which I wooed and lost my darling Donna Anna.

His mind was flooded by poignant memories of geraniums beside a white-washed beach house. He remembered the wonderful mornings, the delicious breakfasts—sausages and strawberries with Donna Anna beside the bluest possible waters, lulled by the sunlight and the pounding surf. He remembered the honey-flavored nights, the delectable midnight rambles along the moonlit beach. Happy though those memories were, he determined to stick to his task and complete his last document.

Now my love belongs forever to that single adorable woman. I will never again give my whole heart to every sweet lollipop the way I once did. Donna Anna owns me and she has run away from me, for no good reason. She has destroyed our happiness and left me only questions. Why did she trample on our perfect bliss? Why were my pleadings of no avail? Why was my most sincere sacrifice to no avail? Why did she flee from our Paradise without a backward glance? Donna Anna has given me my excellently good reason to take the plunge to oblivion, the dive into eternity. Memory, like a veil, obscures my eyesight, worse than my black silk mask ever was. I can no longer see a way to go on in this cold, cruel world.

He reached for his white silk handkerchief. His own prose and pitiful predicament had moved him to tears. He thought, with difficulty, of the pain his beloved might well be suffering. The thought gave him the strength to go on.

I don't know what she is feeling. I think she may be sorry, plowed under by regret. I'd like to think she misses me and that she finds all picnics dry and tasteless after the delicacy of our shared repasts. It would be pretty to think so. But I may never know whether she suffers as I do. That simple maiden to whom I gave my unstinting love may never have appreciated what a rare love she abandoned when she cast me aside.

A tear fell from Don Juan's eye to the page, blurring his words, making a perfect heart-shaped blot on the elegant page. He paused to dry his overflowing eyes and regain his composure.

Donna Anna left me only the ashes of love, left me alone to undergo the bitter pangs of rejection. Others may know this fearsome pain, the awful humiliation of being cast aside by a woman.

> I never had been turned down before that day. My life had been nothing but happiness and love, and the worship of women. All of them always adored me, and I them, until Donna Anna ran from me on that dreadful afternoon. After she left, I wandered the island for days. I was like an orphaned puppy, calling and calling her name. Looking under bushes and into caves, asking after her at the port, in every taverna, asking the tourists as they poured from the cruise ships, inquiring of sailors and old women in the village square, asking them had they seen my Donna Anna. Searching and searching, never finding her.

Don Juan's face reflected the agony of those days in which he wandered over the island, finding out too late that his darling had fled over the sea. The final discovery was too painful for him to write. He was almost done with his note. He wished the unknown reader to feel something of the delicate love that he had enjoyed, the tangible delights of the perfect woman.

> Whoever finds this note, I beg you to keep the vision of that delicious and vanished woman hovering in your memory as she hovers forever in mine. Her image haunts my every waking moment, even more tantalizing to you, who have never seen her, perhaps, than to me, since I enjoyed the bliss as well as the blight. Picture to yourself the dimpled knees of the perfect nude, frolicsome in the sunlight of a tropical island, remember the scent of flowers and seaweed, taste the salt of a warm sea breeze and then imagine that it all revolves around you, that you are at the very heart of this feast for every sense and for the sentiments, that your every movement only increases your delight, that you are never tired, never hungry, never sad, but always bathed in bliss. Did I remember to tell you that her white silk gown flowed over her round sweet behind to her dainty feet so that she looked like a mermaid as she ran away from me? Did I tell you that? Too late now. I am for oblivion.

Don Juan closed the journal and put it on the nightstand, in plain view. He wanted to be sure the proper authorities would find it. Some well-trained, obedient, foolish detective was certain to poke around looking for clues to the fatal act, and would find Don Juan's swan song, his epic of a great love lost for no reason, his final confession. Of course, the plain, ordinary man could never be the same again after reading Don Juan's life story.

The young man smiled, thinking of the pleasure the unknown detective had in store for him, and the secrets of love he would uncover just by reading this slender book. The young man stood up and stretched, his silk pajamas rippling over his sinuous limbs, his resolve firm. He was prepared to die.

"But first," he declared, "one final conquest."

Karl K. Klopfer

Home:
   1234 S. Lennox Avenue
   Waltham, MA 09876
   Telephone: 617-555-7567

Education:
   1966–1971
   St. John's University, Annapolis, MD
   B.S. Fine Arts

   1972–1977
   Yale University
   Ph.D. Clinical Psychology

   1978–1984
   William Alanson White Institute
   Graduated—Psychoanalysis

Experience:
   1984–present
   Clinical Director—New York Hospital
   Treated patients with multiple personality disorders.

Publications:
   Numerous papers for journals on multiple personality disorders.

   Novel: *Creator,* published by Putnam, 1972

   Novel: *Satan,* published by Knopf, 1977

Outside Activities:
   Speaker at professional associations.

*Proposal 2—Bed Ahead: The Complete (but Opinionated) Hostel Ratings Guide**

This proposal's summary includes market research that gives the editor concise and reasonable information about the subject. In place of a contents list, they include lists of their proposed introductory sections and indexes, as well as details of the book's length and organization—all appropriate information for pitching a travel guide like *Bed Ahead.* They follow this with a list of other projected titles, should the publisher be interested in pursuing the whole series; biographical sketches that show their credentials; four sample listings; and a sample introductory section about hostel affiliations.[†]

---

* Evan and Paul followed the recommended Eight Steps and prepared their book proposal—which in this case included a proposal for a series of books in the format of the first one. Well-developed proposal in hand, Evan and Paul researched likely publishers and selected five smaller publishers to whom they sent proposals. Within a month they received three responses from publishers and an attractive offer from one of the Best Bet publishers listed in the Tool Kit section of this book. Their book was accepted by Globe Pequot Press, a major travel publisher.

† This section is not reproduced here.

The Cover Letter

June 1, 2001

Millie Miles
Travel Editor
Globe Pequot Press
6 Business Park Road
Old Saybrook, CT 06475

Dear Millie:

We are writing to propose a unique travel book—the first in a series, we hope, that fills a specific and growing need but, remarkably, has *never been published.* It's called **Bed Ahead: The Complete (but Opinionated) Hostel Ratings Guide, Volume I: United States.**

During our far-flung travels, we have discovered something: hostels aren't just for backpackers anymore. Young, active travelers certainly make up a fast-growing segment of the travel book market. But increasing numbers of *families* use hostels, too, as a way of traveling lightly and affordably. These folks want solid information about safety, cleanliness, and hospitality—and they want to be entertained while reading it. Our guidebook would feature three strengths:

- Being **the first comprehensive guide** to hostels—the first to visit *every* hostel in the U.S., England, France, New Zealand, and so forth.
- **Narrative descriptions** which are fun to read, informative, and go far beyond any existing material on hostels.
- **Standardized ratings,** also never before attempted in a hostel book.

It's a good time for this book. Hostels are booming in popularity (see enclosed marketing research), and they provide affordable, yet interesting, places to stay. A family of four can sleep in a New Mexico teepee or a Georgia tree house for approximately $50. We're certain this U.S. volume has enormous potential for sales—not just to American hikers, bikers, and backpackers, but also to foreign visitors seeking inexpensive, rustic experiences in the United States.

Our credentials, very briefly, are these: one of us has eight years experience as a prize-winning outdoor and travel writer—working for *Sports Illustrated* and *DeLorme Mapping,* among others, while traveling extensively—and the other has visited hostels all over Europe and the U.S. in the course of writing for *Maine Times, AMC Outdoors,* and other publications. We enjoy traveling, work quickly but accurately, and are very committed to completing this book in a timely fashion.

With this letter, you'll find enclosed a complete book proposal, four sample chapters, notes about the potential market, a plan for producing a subsequent line of similar books covering foreign countries, and our CVs.

Thanks very kindly for taking the time to read this. We hope you enjoy the proposal and sample chapters, and we'll talk to you soon.

All our best—

Paul Karr
Evan Halper

The Proposal

Proposal

No publisher has yet produced an informative, detailed guide to hostels—either in the U.S. or abroad. Travelers want information on the *feel* of a place, yet the only remotely complete sources of information on U.S. hostels are two pocket-size booklets of listings: Hostelling International's guide to its member hostels (which are only a fraction of the U.S. total), and a slim, desktop-published pamphlet that adds a list of independent hostels.

But these listings only consist of address, phone number, and price, with perhaps a bit of publicity copy written by the hostels themselves. Also, some hostels advertise in these guides—watering down the books' impact.

What we're proposing is substantially different:

- **We will visit *every* hostel in the U.S.** (and, in subsequent volumes, the UK, France, and so on).
- **We will carefully grade each hostel,** based on our visits and overnight stays.
- **We will write colorful descriptions,** and won't pull punches or plaudits when describing the hostels.

THE POTENTIAL MARKET

Hostels are surprisingly popular. The largest collection of hostels, Hostelling International (HI), claims **four million members worldwide**—and doesn't include hundreds of additional hostels that aren't affiliated with HI. These travelers are the core of our target audience. More numbers:

- HI-affiliated hostels in the U.S. see about **one million overnight visits** each year, and this figure represents less than half the number of visits to *all* U.S. hostels.
- **About one-third of visitors come from the U.S.,** meaning a domestic market of hundreds of thousands.
- **Most HI hostel visitors come from countries** where English is spoken primarily or secondarily:

Germany	110,000 visits/year
England	100,000 visits/year
Australia	90,000 visits/year
Japan	40,000 visits/year
Canada	30,000 visits/year
France	30,000 visits/year
New Zealand	15,000 visits/year

Foreign printings will thus be very important to the success of this book.

- Many hostel visitors are young backpackers, but families and older travelers also use hostels in increasing numbers. The **percentage of elderly hostelers has quadrupled** in the past decade.
- *Good Housekeeping* published a complimentary article on good hostels for families this past March.

INTRODUCTORY MATERIAL

In several introductory sections at the front of the book, we will explain the idea of hostels and the way they operate. Here are some likely section titles:

- a short history of hostels
- about affiliations
- what to expect
- the rating system
- the ten best hostels
- ten to avoid at all costs

We have included one of these sections—"About Affiliations"—with our proposal.

INDEXING

Since the book is organized by region and state, a conventional index won't be necessary. However, we'd like to add a *subjective* index to the back that highlights three or four hostels in each of the following categories:

- most romantic hostels
- best hostels to mountain bike from
- best hostels near major tourist attractions
- most scenic hostels
- best cooking facilities
- best hostel day trips

. . . and so forth.

PROJECTED LENGTH AND ORGANIZATION

We estimate a total of 365 affiliated and unaffiliated hostels in the United States. At one page per entry, plus 15–30 pages of introductory material and section dividers, this works out to at least 380 pages for the first guidebook.

The book would be broken into seven geographical regions; states would be listed alphabetically within region. We would insert rudimentary maps to each region similar to the enclosed example. The regions break out this way:

Chapter 1 CT, ME, MA, NH, VT (no hostels in RI)	**New England**	35 pp
Chapter 2 DC, MD, NJ, NY, PA (none in DE)	**Mid-Atlantic**	45 pp
Chapter 3 AR, GA, FL, KY, LA, MS, NC, SC, TN, VA, WV (none in AL)	**South**	40 pp
Chapter 4 IL, IA, KS, MI, MN, MO, NE, OH, ND, SD, WI (none in IN)	**Midwest**	35 pp
Chapter 5 AZ, CO, NM, TX (none in OK)	**Southwest**	55 pp
Chapter 6 CA, HI, MT, NV, UT, WY	**West**	90 pp
Chapter 7 AK, ID, OR, WA	**Northwest**	60 pp

PROJECTED TIMETABLE

We would spend six months researching and writing the United States edition, and could present a manuscript in **January/February of 2002.** Here is a sample timetable for subsequent volumes covering additional countries:

Title	Published	Updated	Length*
Volume I: United States	spring 2002	yearly	380 pp
Volume II: UK	spring 2002	yearly	390 pp
Volume III: Ireland	spring 2002	yearly	140 pp
Volume IV: France & Spain	fall 2002	every 2 yrs	390 pp

Volume				
Volume VII: Canada & Mexico	fall 2002	every 2 yrs	165 pp	
Volume V: New Zealand	spring 2003	every 2 yrs	290 pp	
Volume VI: Australia	spring 2003	every 2 yrs	305 pp	
Volume VIII: The Mediterranean	spring 2004	every 2 yrs	unknown	
Volume IX: Benelux	spring 2004	every 2 yrs	unknown	
Volume X: Germany, Austria & Switzerland	spring 2004	yearly	unknown	

*includes estimated 10 pages per volume of front matter, maps, and section dividers

CREDENTIALS

PAUL KARR, 33, has worked as a travel and environmental writer for the past 8 years, traveling extensively in the United States and abroad. His prizes include a writing residency at Rocky Mountain National Park outside Denver and a fellowship from the Ludwig-Vogelstein Foundation to write travel essays in Europe. His work has also been featured in *Sports Illustrated, E Magazine,* and *Sanctuary,* among other publications.

EVAN HALPER, 27, has traveled to European and American hostels since he was a boy. Since 1995, he has worked as a staff reporter at *Maine Times,* Maine's largest weekly newspaper, and contributed freelance work to the Appalachian Mountain Club's magazine *AMC Outdoors.*

Sample Entries

Hiram, Maine   A-
Wadsworth Blanchard Farm Hostel
Address: RR2 Box 5992
Phone: (207) 625-7509
Cost: $10 per person
Private rooms: Yes
Affiliation: HI
Office hours: Whenever—just be reasonable. Reservations required.
Extras: Dogs, duck, swing, canoe, occasional rides to and from Portland or Conway

Sally Whitcher calls her cozy getaway in western Maine "a respite for travelers," and it's well worth finding the little village of Hiram just to stay at this place for a night. There's history: the hostel is part of the original farmstead of the Wadsworth family, dating back to the year Gen. Peleg Wadsworth—grandfather of Maine's own Henry Wadsworth Longfellow—first settled the area in 1774.

And there's a relaxed, rustic feel. Whitcher operates a backpacker's heaven with husband Ed Bradley. Both are retired and actively involved in the peace and environmental movements—a pair of idealists committed to the philosophy of hostelling. "I love having people from all nationalities coming and going. It is sort of the epitome of bringing people together and world understanding," she says.

As such, the couple keeps pretty loose rules. Unlike at many hostels, guests are welcome to stay all day if they wish; many do. Georgia and Dakota, the couple's two friendly dogs, are popular among visitors too. Hanging out on the hammock and swings under a shady oak are other favorite diversions, as is spending time with the resident pet duck.

The hostel's design is unusual in that the entire first floor is open, with couches set beside a woodstove and a wide array of books and parlor games. Tapestries and rugs complement the tasteful furnishings and oak walls and floors. Kitchen and dining areas are on the first floor, with two large bedrooms situated upstairs.

Canoeing is the activity of choice in this part of Maine. There is a section of the Ossipee River nearby with class two to three rapids—not much of a whitewater challenge, but a scenic float nonetheless. Rentals cost about $25 per boat.

For a slower pace, you can borrow the hostel's aluminum canoe and visit one of the many local lakes or the meandering Brownfield Bog. Swimming in nearby Stanley Pond is also a good option. Bikers will salivate at the miles of backcountry roads threaded through the local hills, and there are any number of day hikes in the area too, most offering views of the White Mountains. In short: it's hostel heaven.

Crowd	Mellow yellow
Safety	A
Hospitality	A
Cleanliness	A
Ecology	B
Setting	A
Party index	ØØ

{Map Here}

Best ways to get there:

- car: Take Route 25 to Route 160. Go north 1.3 miles to Tripp Town Rd.; then use map.

Conway, New Hampshire   B+
Albert B. Lester Memorial Hostel
Address: 36 Washington Street
Phone: (603) 447-1001
Cost: $16 per person
Private rooms: Yes
Affiliation: HI
Office Hours: 7 a.m.–12 p.m. and 5 p.m.–12 a.m.
Extras: Laundry, TV, free breakfast

The opening last July of this hostel was a monumental event for low-budget travelers. At last, they can take advantage of 750,000 acres of forests, rivers, and mountains in the White Mountains National Forest without dishing out the big bucks for a "quaint" (read: miserable) bed & breakfast.

If it's a green-friendly hostel you want, then this is the place. Everything about this hostel—from the sustainably harvested wooden walls and nontoxic paint to the compost bin in the kitchen—is focused around reducing, reusing, or recycling. A wood chip gasier heats the place; rainwater is collected for certain uses; a wood-burning hot tub is planned; and so on. You get the point.

Sustainability aside, the forty-four-bed farmhouse is a great place to stay. The common room has several couches, there's a gigantic kitchen, and rooms are clean. Most visitors opt to stay in the dorms, divided by sex, but private rooms are available. The layout is a bit sterile, but that's because the hostel is often filled near capacity.

Location is also great. There are two business districts in the Conway area: Conway and North Conway. The latter—complete with tacky outlet stores and fast food chains—bears more resemblance to a strip mall than a secluded paradise. But the hostel is in Conway, a charming village of the *It's a Wonderful Life* ilk. Proprietors Susan Beane and Sophie Barber will help you find the best deals on everything from mountain biking clinics to ice-cream cones to kayak rentals.

The weekend we stayed, the guest list included a half-dozen "gear-heads" in town for a conference on rock climbing. With lots of several-hundred-foot rock faces, the area is world-renowned among rock climbers. If you are into that kind of thing, be sure to catch one of the hostel's Friday night slide shows. Presentations vary, but often focus on the most extreme sorts of life-threatening outdoor enjoyment.

Biggest setback? The only other hostel accessible from here by public transportation is in Boston. Maine is trying to acquire an abandoned rail line that stretches from Portland to near Conway, so someday it might be possible to take the train; for now, though, it's car, bike, or thumb. Hitching is commonplace and biking is also possible, but car traffic from Portland is heavy, with no real shoulder.

Crowd	Gearheads galore
Safety	B
Hospitality	B
Cleanliness	A
Ecology	A
Setting	A
Party index	ØØ

{Map Here}

Best ways to get there:

- car: Take U.S. 302 to Route 16; follow into Conway village; then use map.
- bus: From Boston, Vermont Transit makes one trip per day ($22 one-way).

Savannah, Georgia   B
Savannah International Youth Hostel
304 East Hall Street
Savannah, GA 31401
Phone: (912) 236-7744
Cost: $11 per person
Private rooms: Yes (1)
Affiliation: None
Office hours: 7–10 a.m. and 5–11 p.m. Don't bother trying during the day.
Extras: Ping-Pong, foosball, TV, rides to or from airport (sometimes)

It's impossible to fault the location of this hostel: set smack in the middle of Savannah's justly famous historic district, the place is only a short walk from living history. Housed in one of those gorgeous old antebellum mansions you always see in the movies, the whitewashed Savannah hostel is a fine place to crash but really too small to hang around for long. That's fine, because there's so much to see in Savannah and the nearby beaches of Tybee Island.

"This is a fantastic place to visit on foot," says hostel manager Brian Sherman, 29, a Miami native who bought the house in 1988 and converted it to a hostel.

There's a new supermarket right across the street, so finding food isn't a problem. The tiny kitchen gets awfully crowded sometimes; however, it's a nice place to share breakfast stories, but fixing dinner can be somewhat irritating as a line of backpackers queue up for dishes, stove space, and the rest. There can be a wait for the bathrooms, too, which are reasonably clean.

After dark, Brian sometimes wanders upstairs to play a mean game of Ping-Pong or foosball. He also offers good (if perfunctory) directions around town. For several years, he has planned to construct additional apartments for couples and families.

The bad stuff? It's occasionally possible you won't be able to find a room here, especially in spring, when tourists descend on the flowery city *en masse*—and Girl Scouts make pilgrimages from all over the nation. (The founder's home and headquarters are a block or two away.) It's a good idea to call ahead a day or two just to make sure there will be room at the inn.

A more serious warning: the hostel itself is very secure, but this neighborhood of Savannah has had a few crime problems in recent years. Don't set out alone from the hostel on foot at night, stay in well-lit areas, and you should be fine.

Crowd	Aussie burnouts and giggly Girl Scouts
Safety	B
Hospitality	A
Cleanliness	C
Ecology	C
Setting	A
Party index	ØØØ

{Map Here}

Best way to get there:

- car: Drive I-95 to Savannah; take Exit 17 to I-16 East, then follow map.
- plane: Small airport 7 miles from hostel. Nearest large airport: Jacksonville (2 hours).
- rail: Amtrak to Richmond Hill (15 miles away); take shuttle bus.
- bus: Greyhound stops downtown.

Québec City, Québec　　　B
Centre International de Séjour de Québec
(Québec City International Hostel)
Address: 19 rue Sainte-Ursule
Phone: (418) 694-0755
Cost: $15 Canadian (about $12 U.S.) per person
Private room: Yes
Affiliation: HI
Office hours: 11 a.m.–2 a.m.
Extras: Small travel supply shop, laundry, cafeteria, vending machines, TV

Québec City's big, dorm-like hostel draws a young crowd, and as a result it can get noisy. The level of noise depends on your luck of the draw; with 300 beds, you might be in a quiet, family-oriented wing—or land straight in Beer-Breath Central.

Rooms are fine, though the walls are paper-thin. The unisex bathrooms are reasonably clean, and there's a spacious cafeteria (we didn't try the food). But the dining room and kitchen, while well-equipped, are simply too tiny for such a huge hostel. It isn't odd to find a half-dozen or more solitary students hanging out, reading dog-eared classics while simultaneously flouting *both* the no-smoking and no-drinking rules. Meanwhile, families with children dance around and between in a desperate attempt to get the dinner cooked.

In spite of the hostel's high activity level, you won't need to spend much time there, because its surroundings are very hard to beat. At your feet is North America's oldest city (and its only walled city): you can actually sit on top of the old ramparts, eating and looking out on the gorgeous Saint Lawrence. The hostel is perfectly situated, just steps from grocery stores, crépe shops, churches, pubs, a riverwalk and lots of obligatory tourist stops.

Québec's nightlife is thus very lively—the food and drink is as good as any in North America—so travelers take advantage of it. Hostel doors are supposed to close at 2 a.m., but since you can still get let in afterward, it's safe to assume people will be coming and going for a good part of the evening. Most of the crowd will have come from elsewhere in Canada, but there might also be fussy English families grousing about the noise. Surprisingly, not many Americans find their way here.

You won't need to worry about crime, but parking can be tricky. Try to grab a street spot near the hostel as early in the day as possible, as you won't need your car. Or park in one of the bizarre private parking lots that look like Roman stadiums.

Crowd	English nannies and pub-crawling Canadian dandies
Safety	B
Hospitality	C
Cleanliness	B
Ecology	B
Setting	A
Party index	ØØØØØ

{Map Here}

Best ways to get there:

- car: Drive Autoroute 73 until Exit 9; take Chemin Saint-Louis into city, then use map.
- plane: Small airport 10 miles from hostel. Nearest large airport: Montreal (2 hours).

Summary

After reading this chapter, you should feel that you have been invited into a special seminar and been able to share with successful authors their secrets of success. Some of what you have read will be very useful to you—and some not at all. If you are able to use one idea or concept to make your proposal more effective, your time will have been well spent.

At the heart of this chapter is the advice: *never submit an entire manuscript.* An editor only samples manuscripts. Why allow her to choose a portion of your book at random? Instead, develop a proposal that takes the editor where you want her to go, describes your book quickly and deftly, and hopefully leads to a positive response. Provide enough information to give the editor a representative sample of how effectively you write and the organization of your ideas. This system of providing "just enough" succeeds because deep down, editors enjoy the thrill of discovering a new author and a good book. The talented editor wishes to be part of the creative process and establish a bond with you as you work on the book together. Submit enough of the manuscript to encourage her to participate with you in making your manuscript publishable.

8

The Editor and the First-Time Author Negotiate

Think positively! Be prepared to receive a call from an editor who has read your nonfiction proposal, or the summary of your novel, and loves it. She will invite you in to talk about your book (if convenient) and will then make an offer to acquire the rights to your work.* This offer is usually verbal and covers the essential terms of her proposal: the advance payment, the royalty, and whether the book will be a hardcover or paperback (or both). This is followed by the publisher's standard contract.

Most editors prefer to deal with an agent rather than directly with the author because a reasonably competent agent knows the "rules of the road" and speaks the same language. The editor has dual roles—she is both a sympathetic editor and a businessperson representing the publisher—and she would like to keep those roles separate. Often, however, the author may negotiate on her own. For first-time authors the money involved is often modest, and

---

*Publishers do not "buy" books. They acquire the rights to publish in the territory agreed on with the author and to license subsidiary rights to third parties on their behalf and on behalf of the author. The rights licensed may be sales in territories outside the U.S. and Canada, translation into foreign languages, etc. For a more complete explanation, see Chapter 9.

some good agents will not accept a beginning author unless he believes the author will be productive in the future. Other agents who do accept new authors do not always spend sufficient time making the best deal possible. An author negotiating for herself should, if at all possible, have a lawyer represent her, specifically a lawyer who is familiar with publishing and knows the deal-making side of the industry. In any case, the first-time author should assist her representative by understanding the business and contract terms (Chapters 8 and 9 will help in this area). A knowledgeable client who is familiar with the realities of the publishing marketplace is a blessing to an agent, a lawyer . . . and the editor as well.

While most good agents know the publisher's contracts and are experienced negotiators, a lawyer who is familiar with publishing is very helpful. The publishing contract is a transfer of valuable rights from the author to the publisher, usually for her entire life and for seventy years thereafter. Both the publisher and the author obligate themselves to perform for the benefit of each other. A lawyer is important to ensure that the transfer of intellectual property, your valuable asset, is completed in accordance with the Copyright Act.

While the first confirmation that your book will be published may come in a telephone call or a letter, the negotiation that precedes the drafting of a formal contract usually takes place in the editor's office. The editor has been provided with, or has developed on her own, a financial analysis that sets out the expected sales and returns, a tentative retail price, a manufacturing cost based on an estimate of the book's length and cost of typesetting, cover art, illustrations, if any, and overhead expenses. The financial director, in developing a system estimating profit or loss on a book, may provide standard percentages for sales, fulfillment, and other overhead costs to simplify the editor's analysis.

The actual "profit and loss" may be more complicated, but in general, this is what the editor might have as a financial guide:

The First Novel
by A. A. Author

75,000 words—Pub. Date Fall 2002—no illustrations	
Estimated Retail Price	$25
Average Discount*	45%
Average Net Price Received per Book	$13.75
Gross Unit Sales Life of Book	30,000
Less Returns 33^1/$_3$%	10,000
Net Unit Sales	20,000
Net Receipts	$275,000
Mfg. Cost—Variable and Fixed	$120,000
Overhead (35% of Net Receipts)	$96,250
Total Mfg. & Overhead	$216,250
Net before Royalty & Profit	$58,750
Profit Target (15% of Net Receipts)	$41,250
Available for Advance and Royalty	$17,500

There are a number of methods to arrive at what the publisher believes he can afford to offer as an advance payment and royalty, and this is just one. Based on this example, however, the publisher would offer a $17,500 advance payment, probably one-half on signing the contract, and one-half on delivery of a satisfactory manuscript. In this case, the publisher is proposing to make an advance payment based upon his estimate of net sales for the life of the edition.

Although a royalty scale starting at 10 percent of the retail price and escalating to 15 percent is fairly standard in trade publishing, the author might be offered a low 6 percent royalty based on *net* receipts,

---

*This is the amount by which the retail price is reduced or "discounted" when sold to a retailer or wholesaler. The resulting number is the average the publisher's customers (the booksellers) pay to the publisher. Thus, in this model, an average bookseller pays $13.75 to the publisher for a book. The discount is computed from the *recommended retail price established by the publisher,* not a discounted retail price that the retailer might establish on his own.

the money the publisher receives from sales after it discounts the book. If the 20,000 unit net sales are achieved as projected, the author would receive $16,500 (6 percent of $275,000) in royalties, slightly less than shown in the preceding chart. A 6 percent royalty on *net* receipts is low, even for a first-time author, but to increase it would mean the publisher must accept less profit, fail to recover his over-head, or have to rely on income from subsidiary rights sales. (According to statistics prepared by the American Association for Publishers, most trade publishers fail to make a profit on their own sales and depend on sales of subsidiary rights to make a profit. Books with mass market paperback sales potential are sought after by editors.) The author, however, also receives a share of the subsidiary rights. For example, if the hardcover book were sold for publication as a mass market paperback, the author would receive more money, usually 50 percent of the amount the publisher receives.

Most publishers base their royalty on the "cover price" or rec-ommended retail price. For example, net sales of 20,000 copies at recommended retail price of $25 would result in retail sales of $500,000; 6 percent of $500,000 would provide a royalty of $30,000. Basing the royalty on a percentage of *net* receipts rather than on a percentage of the cover price reduces the royalty to the author by almost half.

Net Receipts	$275,000
6% of Net Payment to Author	$16,500
Retail Sales	$500,000
6% of Retail Payment to Author	$30,000

Now comes the negotiation. You, the author, are not aware of the financial analysis in the hands of the editor, and when you hear the proposal, the royalty may sound low to you. The editor also knows that the royalty is low but must be guided by financial analysis.

Let's assume you had heard that the standard hardcover royalties were:

10% of *retail* (not net) price on the first 5,000 net
(i.e., after returns) copies sold,

12^1/$_2$% of *retail* (not net) price on the next 5,000
    copies sold, and

15% thereafter.

The editor is in a tough spot dealing directly with the author. She wants to maintain her relationship with the author, sometimes feeling closer to the author than to the publishing house, but her duty is to try to make a deal that is fair to her employer. The first-time author, even knowing this is an offer well below the royalty rate paid to established authors, does not wish to "blow" the deal, and so she is tentative about pressing her newly learned but imperfect knowledge. Often a third party is needed to encourage the editor to build an economic foundation for a better deal.

An experienced publishing lawyer can be very valuable in bridging this gap. Unlike those of an agent, the services of attorneys are readily available; they charge by the hour and assist in the negotiation of the deal and execution of the contract. It is likely that the additional money a publishing lawyer will generate in increased royalties and other concessions will pay for all or part of his fee. The publishing lawyer should know the economic rules of the road for advances and royalties for the genre of your book (romance novels, children's books, fiction and nonfiction for adults). If the lawyer can improve the money aspects of the contract and the book is successful, he will provide a better economic foundation for future deals. When the author starts with a lower than normal royalty rate and advance, it is difficult to improve the economics for subsequent books.

Since I am a lawyer, you may think that my advice to seek a publishing lawyer to represent you is self-serving. Not true. Some of the clients whom I have represented are CEOs of major corporations who have negotiated million- and even billion-dollar deals on their own in their respective industries but realized they needed a publishing lawyer to negotiate their book deal. There is a list of intellectual property law firms shown in *LMP* and you should seek out a knowledgeable attorney, whether from *LMP* or on your own, to represent you. If you cannot find a lawyer where you live, you can use an out-of-town lawyer and communicate with him through faxes and telephone calls.

If you cannot engage the services of a lawyer, you should understand the editor's constraints, and try gently to move the advance and royalty rate up. Negotiating alone is not recommended; nevertheless, here is some advice that will be helpful.

As a first move, try to convince the editor that the book is likely to sell additional copies, especially if sales figures of similar books are available. Then point out that most authors receive escalating royalty rates of 10, 12^1/$_2$, and 15 percent. Suggest those areas of income from subsidiary rights sales (book clubs, foreign rights, etc.) that might provide more money to the publisher. Your objective is to introduce into the equation sources for additional income, either from larger than estimated retail sales or subsidiary rights, and to point to the "normal" royalty rates.

Realize there is always give-and-take in negotiation. If the editor balks at changing the sales estimate, which would increase the advance, seek a higher royalty rate because the existing rate based on net receipts rather than the publisher's recommended retail price is at the low end of the scale. The editor may prefer to increase the royalty rate rather than increase the advance payment, since royalty rates based upon the retail prices are "standard." Have your calculator handy and ask the editor to explain what income you might expect under various royalty rates; the numbers will demonstrate how the lower royalty rate affects your income and will help you negotiate the best deal possible.

If you are concerned about making the best deal possible *and* maintaining your relationship with the editor, ask her to level with you and show you how she can improve the deal and still get it approved by her management. Most editors will help the first-time author, especially if they hope to publish subsequent books. But remember the editor works for the "house."

These are the money issues to be negotiated. The most important remaining points to be negotiated are the grant of rights, territories into which the publisher can sell the book, and the division of subsidiary rights income. I have outlined guidelines for a poor, fair, and good deal* in the hardcover fiction and nonfiction market that you can use in studying the deal you are offered. Royalties and advances are substantially different and lower for children's books, original mass market and trade paperbacks, and some reference books. One technique to establish the fairness of the offer made to you is to ask the editor how this offer compares with the average or best offer she has made. She will usually tell you the truth, and explain why, if true, your offer is less than the other offers.

Before considering the deal terms, there is one serious defining issue. In some instances, especially in nonfiction books, publishers will submit a "work-for-hire" contract. This is a "no-no." Such a contract conveys all rights to the publisher. The author, even though she may receive a royalty and a share of subsidiary rights, is not the owner of the copyright. If you are confronted with such a contract it is a poor deal.

---

*These deals originally appeared in *How To Be Your Own Literary Agent* by Richard Curtis. The author has recently modified the deals to bring them up to date. If the terms used are confusing, come back to this after you have read Chapter 9, or look for definitions in PubSpeak (Appendix A).

A Poor Deal

- Hardcover advance is under $5,000.
- Hardcover royalties under 10% on first 5,000, 12$^1/_2$% next 5,000, and 15% thereafter based upon recommended retail price. (An even worse deal is the offer of an outright payment with no royalty.)
- Royalties based on the net receipts of the publisher.
- Trade paperback royalties under 6% with no higher rate of royalty on increasing sales.
- Mass market royalties are under 6% with no higher royalty breaks (there's usually one at 150,000 copies).
- World rights in all languages. (For original romance paperbacks, this is acceptable if the author's share of foreign rights is 50%–75%.)
- Publisher gets more than 25% of British and translation revenue and more than 15% of income on first serial rights.
- Publisher gets participation in movie and television revenue.
- Publisher gets more than 50% of subsidiary rights income (book club, paperback, etc.).
- Publisher insists on audio and all new technology rights, including online and e-book rights, without a clear compensation schedule.

A Fair Deal

- Hardcover advance is $20,000–$30,000.

- Hardcover royalties are 10% of retail cover price on first 5,000 copies, $12^1/2$% on next 5,000, and 15% thereafter.

- Trade paperback royalties are $7^1/2$%–8% of retail cover price.

- Mass market royalties are at least 6% of cover price on first 150,000 copies, 8% thereafter.

- English language rights in the U.S. and Canada, U.S. territories and possessions.

- British and translation rights subject to author's approval, with author receiving 75% of income received by publisher when the publisher licenses the rights.

- Publisher keeps only 10% of first serial rights.

- Publisher has no rights in movies or television deals.

- Publisher shares all subsidiary publishing rights income, including new technology rights, with author on a 50-50 basis.

A Good Deal

- Hardcover advance is over $20,000.

- Hardcover royalties are 10% of the retail cover price on the first 5,000 copies sold, $12^1/2$% on the next 5,000 copies, and 15% thereafter.

- Trade paperback royalties are more than $7^1/2$% of retail cover price, with royalty break points to 10%.

- Mass market royalties are more than 6% on first 150,000 copies; 8% thereafter.

- English language rights in the U.S. and Canada, U.S. territories and possessions.

- British and translation rights subject to author's approval, with author receiving 75% of publisher's income; if publisher does not license rights in two years, rights revert to author.

- Author retains first serial rights.

- Publisher has no rights in movies or television deals.

- Publisher may license audio and new technology, with 50% each on first $150,000, 60% to author on all income over $150,000. Payment of money received from paperback publisher to be paid by hardcover publisher to author thirty days after receipt, provided advance has been recovered.

- Income from book clubs and other subsidiary rights sales shared equally and paid thirty days after receipt, provided the advance has been recovered.

- Royalty rates for e-books at 35% to 50% of publisher's net receipt.

None of these terms are set in stone, and these deals are only meant to serve as rough guidelines in your negotiation. Most trade publisher-author contracts have terms that fall within the ambit of the Fair Deal. Favored authors and those with good track records receive all or a significant portion of the terms in the Good Deal category.

You can now keep abreast of the deals being offered to authors by publishers by subscribing (no fee) to www.caderbooks.com. This service reports the deals being offered by publishers to authors.

Some authors are so happy to be published, they will accept an offer that is much too low and affects their future deals adversely. Do not be afraid to argue for a better deal. Remember that the editor, having come this far, really wants to publish your book. Be gently persuasive and persistent, but don't expect to receive everything you ask for on your first book. Your goal should be to achieve slightly more than the Poor Deal on your first book, move up the ladder and get a Fair Deal or better on the next book, and then get Good Deals for future books. It could happen.

9

Creating Contract Literacy

Unfortunately, after the editor has paid the author the greatest possible compliment by offering to publish her book, sometimes the author's joy can turn to sadness or, at the least, confusion when the author reads the publisher's "standard" book contract—eight or more pages printed in small type resembling a landlord lease and full of legal-sounding, difficult-to-understand terms. (Most of the text is "boilerplate," a legal term for the terms that are fairly standard on one publisher's contract.) Both sides know the "standard" contract is not standard. It can be revised if the author is a savvy negotiator and knows her rights and has some negotiation leverage.

In its most poetic form, a contract is a "promise" for a "promise." The author promises to deliver a book, carefully described, at a given date, which is her own work, and if the book is satisfactory the publisher agrees to print, publish, and distribute the book and pay the author money.

The publisher uses a long-form contract to protect his economic position and to cover contingencies that might arise. In agreeing to publish, he commits substantial sums of money and time. On her side, the author has already invested a year or more of her time in the book and wishes to ensure that the publisher will do his job. At the end of the day, business terms should be included in a contract that will enable both parties to be protected if they understand the "rules of the road."

This chapter is designed to help you, the author, develop contract literacy—to familiarize you with copyright law, explain legal terms, define the issues you will meet in the standard contract, and show you how to seek changes for your benefit. Most publishers prefer to have the author represented by an agent or attorney, who will review the contract on behalf of the author. Since the publisher's contract was drafted by a lawyer and the editor has a lawyer available, the law offers protection in some instances to a party to a contract who is not represented by a lawyer. Where a publisher's contract is unfair and where the author is not represented by a lawyer, should a dispute arise, the courts will often see that justice is done for the author.

If you are a published author, you should join The Authors Guild (31 East 28th Street, New York, NY 10016). The Guild has seminars to assist authors in negotiating their publishing contracts and provides many other services. You can find The Authors Guild on the Web at www.authorsguild.org.

When your book has been selected by an editor and the business terms worked out, it's almost a sure thing you will agree on a contract. However, as I have said before, no contract should be signed without the advice of a lawyer or agent familiar with publishing contracts and the Copyright Act. A good lawyer who knows publishing will not "blow" the deal or antagonize the publisher. He will make a deal fair to both sides consistent with the law. If you become contract literate, you will save yourself time and money when you understand the issues and can respond sensibly to your lawyer.

A lawyer is especially valuable if you are offered a "work-for-hire" contract. As indicated previously, generally this is a "no-no," and it will take the knowledge and the persuasive ability of a lawyer to argue that you are entitled to a standard author publisher agreement in which you license the rights to the publisher and retain the copyright.

Some publishers often have different standard contracts for paperback and trade, juvenile books, reference books, and so on. The essential terms are identical, since copyright law applies to all publishing contracts, but certain business terms may vary.

While, as you will see, there are many subordinate issues to be addressed, the main issues to be negotiated are the rights to be conveyed and money.

Grant of Rights

Under the current Copyright Act, the author is the proprietor (owner) of all rights in the literary work (the right to license the work as a book) and the owner of all derivative rights. This is not a single right but a bundle of rights, owned by the author, starting with literary rights, including film and dramatic rights and a long list of potential uses of the literary work in other forms that are called derivative rights.

The author may grant all or any one of the rights; however, an exclusive grant *must be in writing*. Each right can be sold separately, but in real life, most of the rights that relate to the exploitation of the literary rights are sold together in a single transaction. Any right not granted in writing is automatically retained by the author. Beware of the use of the term "volume rights," sometimes used to describe the rights granted. This term is used primarily in the United Kingdom and is a grant of all print rights, hardcover or softcover. The "writing" required to make an exclusive grant of rights can be as informal as a paper napkin used at the luncheon table where the deal is completed as long as the basic terms of the deal are written and signed by the parties. However, the "writing" is much more likely to be a multipage document prepared by the publisher and submitted to the author after the author has verbally accepted the offer made by the publisher in a letter or by telephone.

The author's rights to be granted can be organized under "Form," "Language," "Territory," and "Time."

Form

Generally, the author grants rights to "print, publish, and distribute a book." The book should be identified by its actual or working title and a short description of the content. Most trade book publishers publish only in hardcover and trade paperback form. (The trade paperback is about the same size as the hardcover but has paper covers.) It is industry practice to grant both hardcover and trade paperback rights since almost all publishers have trade paperback lines. As you will see when payment terms are discussed, each type of book carries its own measure of author compensation.

Most hardcover publishers do not publish mass market paperbacks on their own. (There are major trade publishers who own mass market paperback publishing houses and offer deals for both hardcover and mass market paperback book rights in a single contract.) As we discussed previously, publishers who do not own mass market paperback houses will seek to have the author grant them the right to license the book to a publisher whose sole business is the publication of mass market paperbacks. The mass market edition usually appears one year after publication of the hardcover book. The rationale developed by hardcover publishers, to support their position in seeking to obtain and license mass market paperback rights, is that the hardcover edition of the book establishes reader acceptance that can then be exploited by the mass market paperback publisher. Because of his work and investment in launching the book, the hardcover publisher contends he should share the income from the paperback publication with the author. This concept is generally accepted, and it is normal for the author to grant the hardcover publisher the right to license the paperback and share the income, normally on a 50-50 basis. Major authors often command a larger share of the paperback income.

Most authors grant the hardcover publisher the right to license book club rights, and the income received from book club sales is almost always shared equally.

The normal grant language that the author should expect to see in the contract should read:

> The author hereby grants and assigns to the publisher the sole and exclusive rights to publish a work entitled "The Merry Month of May," a romantic novel of approximately 100,000 words, in hardcover and trade paperback under terms and conditions set forth below. The author also grants to the publisher the right to license others to publish and distribute the work in the form and under the terms as set forth under Subsidiary Rights in paragraph ____.

This language grants the hardcover and trade paperback rights to the publisher and authorizes the publisher to license other rights as specified, which would include the mass market paperback and book club rights as well as some other rights which are described later. If language contained in the standard contract is reasonably close to this sample, the author should be willing to accept it.

Language

English-language rights may be granted to the U.S. publisher. Some authors will retain the English-language rights for the United Kingdom and then employ an agent to sell these rights directly to a British publisher. The major differences in a grant occur in the grant of translation rights. Publishing is an international business and foreign-language rights are important and valuable. The publisher will seek to obtain translation rights for as many countries as possible. If the publisher has the ability to sell rights abroad on his own or through an agent, these rights should be granted by the author with a provision that would enable her to recover these rights if, after two or three years, the rights are not sold and translation has not commenced. (Well-established authors often retain the foreign translation rights and use an agent who specializes in selling foreign rights to sell them, allowing the author to keep all the income less the agent's commission.)

Language in the contract similar to the sample below is appropriate for a first-time author:

> The author grants the right to the publisher to publish the work in English and to translate or arrange for translation of the work in the following languages: *(list)*
>
> In the event, after two years from the date of the initial publication of the work in English, a contract has not been executed with a foreign publisher for publication in a language set forth above, the right to publish in that language will automatically revert to the author. Any contract or translation must provide for publication of the translated work not later than eighteen months after signing of the translation contract. All such contracts require the author's prior approval, which will not be unreasonably withheld.

In these typical paragraphs, the author has provided the publisher with the opportunity to realize additional income from the sale of translation rights which, of course, he will share with the author. If the publisher cannot arrange for a translation, the rights revert to the author and she has a chance to find someone to exploit the uncommitted rights. The sample paragraph also protects the author by requiring timely publication of the translated edition and her prior approval.

Territory

Since the author has granted the rights for publication in English, and English is a principal language in many countries, the territory in which the English-language book can be sold must be delineated. The most restrictive territory allocation is:

> The author grants the publisher the right to print, publish, and distribute the English-language edition of the work in *the United States, its territories and possessions, and Canada.*

The author may substitute broader territorial grants for the italicized portions. (The only issue is the ability of the publisher to exploit the rights in the territories granted by the author.) Some publishers will seek a territorial designation as *"English-language editions of the work throughout the world."* The reason for the publisher seeking an expanded grant is that there are large English-language markets outside the United States and Canada—the United Kingdom, Australia, and Europe, where English is often a second language.

Once again, the question to be asked is, "Can the publisher exploit this territory either on his own or by licensing his rights to another publisher?" In most instances, and especially now that there is a common market in Europe, the United States publisher will sublicense his English-language rights to a U.K. publisher. It is difficult for the author, especially the first-time author, to substitute her judgment for the publisher's, even one with limited overseas contacts. If the author does grant world English-language rights, she should reserve the right of reversion if contracts to exploit these rights are not entered into in a reasonable period of time.

Workable compromise language, as follows, could be accepted by the author:

> The author grants the publisher English-language rights throughout the world. It is the publisher's intention to enter into a contract for English-language publication in the United Kingdom, Australia, and new Zealand for sales of English-language books in these territories. In the event a contract is not entered into within one year after publication in the United States, the rights for publication in any country in which a contract has not been executed will revert to the author. Contracts for exploitation of these rights are

subject to the author's prior approval, which shall not be unreasonably withheld.

Time

Rarely is there a grant for less than the term of the copyright, which is currently the author's life and seventy years thereafter. The Authors Guild has campaigned to have authors limit their initial grant to a term of twenty years, which would allow the author to recover and resell her rights upon the expiration of the term. The current copyright law provides for the right of the author to recover her book within a five-year period beginning in the thirty-fifth year. Thus, even under a grant for the life of the copyright, the author can recover her rights in a shorter term. The time and energy it would take to negotiate a shorter term for the hardcover or trade paperback is usually not worth the benefit likely to be achieved.

The shorter term is important when a license has been entered into by the hardcover publisher with a publisher of mass market paperback books. A successful mass market paperback might sell a substantial number of copies each year over an extended period. If the hardcover publisher, on behalf of the author, has the right to terminate the agreement after a seven- or ten-year term while the book is still selling well, the paperback publisher, who is generally interested in retaining the book, will pay an additional advance payment and royalty to be able to retain the book on his list. If not, there may be other publishers who would be interested in acquiring the steady-selling mass market paperback rights and might outbid the original mass market publisher. The trade press reports the resale of rights and renewals on a regular basis. One world-class author whose paperbacks sell in the millions was well advised early in his career and limited the term of his paperback license to seventeen years. Because his books were very successful, he was able to renegotiate, when the seventeen-year term was almost over, some of the contracts on his early books with large additional advances.

Since many of the contracts for mass market paperback books are negotiated by the hardcover publisher, on his own behalf and on behalf of the author, the author should retain the right of approval of this and other contracts to be certain that all the terms including the grant period for the mass market paperback is significantly shorter than the life of the copyright. While it is not usual practice, the author might try to insert a sentence under the subsidiary rights provision to this effect:

> In licensing rights for mass market paperback books, the life of the license granted by the publisher shall not exceed ten years. All such contracts shall be submitted by the publisher for prior approval to the author, whose approval shall not be unreasonably withheld.

Sometimes, since the publisher has a strong bargaining position vis-à-vis the first-time author, she might expect to see in rare instances a contract provision like this:

> The author hereby grants the publisher the sole and exclusive right to publish in **volume** form in all languages throughout the world for the full term of the copyright as may now or thereafter exist the work, "The Merry Month of May," a novel of approximately 100,000 words together with any revised editions thereof, together with the following sub-sidiary rights: [*the contract provision then lists eighteen separate rights concluding with* "any right not in existence now which may come into being in the future."]

In the illustration shown above, the author would effectively convey all her rights for her lifetime and seventy years thereafter. The words *volume rights* as they appear in this paragraph are what the lawyers call a term of art, which the courts have determined to mean all formats . . . hardcover, softcover, in short, any way the book can be reproduced and distributed. A first-time author, or even experienced authors, *should resist this grant of rights because it is serious overreaching by the publisher.*

Money

Income from Advances

The author will be paid by the publisher for the exploitation of the rights transferred, by receiving royalties, some part of which is pre-paid or "advanced." This is how the term *advance* crept into the language of publishing. (Originally the publisher intended the author to live on the advance while she wrote the book.) An advance is usually paid to the author by the publisher in installments: a portion on signing of the contract, perhaps another portion on submission of a segment of the manuscript, and a final portion on receipt of a "satisfactory manuscript." Advances may be paid in two installments for modest advances or, where there are huge advances, in ten annual installments. It is common for a modest advance to be paid half on signing and half on delivery of a satisfactory manuscript. Payments for larger advances are often paid one-third on signing, one-third on delivery of a satisfactory manuscript, and one-third on publication.

The publisher conditions all advance payments upon the submission of a *satisfactory manuscript,* a concept that is over a hundred years old and that has been redefined by many recent court decisions. If the publisher rejects the manuscript as unsatisfactory, the contract usually provides for the advance to be repaid by the author to the publisher and the manuscript returned to the author. Repayment can be made either out of the author's current funds or from the proceeds she receives from a subsequent sale of the manuscript. However, the contract must state clearly the source from which the funds are to be repaid if the manuscript is unsatisfactory. Most publishers will set a deadline for third-party publication if they allow a first-proceeds clause. If the author does not sell her publication within the time allowed, the publisher will require the author to repay the advance from her own funds.

If the author fails to deliver a manuscript in a timely manner, the contract will normally provide for the advance to be repaid by the author. More about this later.

Income from Royalties

The publisher also agrees to pay a royalty as compensation for the rights conveyed by the author. This royalty is normally a percentage of the suggested retail price, but can be based on net receipts. (Royalty rates are generally, but not always, computed using the publisher's suggested price as the base. The fact that the retail price of the book is discounted by a retailer has no effect on this compensation.) For example, a royalty of 10 percent of the suggested retail price of twenty dollars set by the publisher requires that the publisher pay the author two dollars for each book sold at retail. Royalty rates can escalate as the unit sales increase. The theory that dictates the practice of escalating royalties is that the publisher's plant costs are largest for the initial publication and the author should share this expense by receiving a lower royalty until these costs are recovered.

On a hardcover trade book, the rates of royalty are generally:

On sales of the first 5,000 copies   10% of retail
On sales of the next 5,000 copies $12^{1}/_{2}$% of retail
On all sales over 10,000 copies   15% of retail

Trade paperback royalties are lower—usually $7^{1}/_{2}$ to 10 percent, sometimes even lower.

Mass market paperback royalties are generally from 6 to 8 percent, except for major authors who may be able to command multi-million-dollar advances and larger percentage royalty payments.

Children's books usually remain at 10 percent of retail until the sales reach 20,000 or 25,000 copies.

Income from Subsidiary Rights

The publisher also agrees to pay a percentage of the money received from licensing the subsidiary rights of the book. These amounts vary by the license granted. This is a typical division of income:

Right Sold	% to Author
Sale of mass market paperback reprint	50%
Book clubs	50%
First serial rights (sale to a magazine prior to publication; often retained by the author)	90%
Second serial rights (sale to magazine after publication)	50%
Microfilm rights	50%
Selections and abridgments	50%
Electronic rights (if sold within two years of signing the contract)	50%
Foreign publication license Outside U.S.	75%
Other rights	
Audio	75%
Translation	75%
*Dramatic	75%
*Movie and television	75%
*Merchandising	75%

The rights for performance and merchandising shown with asterisks should not be granted to the publisher. These rights may be a major source of income for the author and the publisher is usually not well equipped to sell them. The best advice to an author, new or established, is to retain dramatic and merchandising rights. Publishers have excellent subsidiary rights departments that sell most rights very effectively, but selling a book for a film or play or selling the rights for games or T-shirts requires agents who specialize in these fields. However, if your publisher insists on sharing in these rights, he should receive no more than an agent, typically 10 to 15 percent of the money realized from the sale.

The newest important rights, electronic rights and other new, often yet-to-be-defined technologies, raise issues still being debated by authors and publishers. (The Authors Guild Web site presents some interesting materials on this subject.) Some publishers who have made substantial investments in creating e-books deserve the author's support by a grant of these rights to the publisher at the prevailing royalty rates that range from 35 to 50 percent of net receipts. The publisher should be given a limited time to exploit the new technology rights, and then, if they are not exploited by the publisher, the rights should be reverted to the author, for her exploitation.

Method of Payment

In consideration for the grant of the rights, the author receives an advance payment—a lump sum, which may be paid in one or more installments as a prepayment of royalties. During the course of the contract, the author earns royalties based on the retail sales of the book and income from the various subsidiary rights. As royalties and other income are earned, they are charged against the advance. If earnings do not exceed the amount of the advance, most contracts provide that the advance payment is not recoverable. The contract should make this clear by identifying it as an "unrecoverable advance."

Despite the fact that every publisher, large and small, uses computers, the publishers make accountings to authors only twice a year followed by a ninety-day delay in payment. For example, a typical trade publisher will close his royalty accounts on October 31 and send the author a check based on the October 31 balance on January 31. This long delay has withstood attack from The Authors Guild, and it is changed only for major authors if the contract provides that large sums such as advances from paperback houses must be paid thirty or sixty days after receipt. A royalty statement sent by the publisher to the author will look in simplest terms something like this:

Royalty Statement
for _____ as of _____

DOMESTIC NET SALES FOR THE PERIOD

Unit Sales	Retail	% of Retail	Due Author
5,000	$20.00	10	$10,000
3,000	$20.00	$12^1/_2$	$7,500

Total **Domestic Sales** 8,000			$17,500

SUBSIDIARY RIGHTS

Income Payment from Book Club $10,000 Total (your share $5,000)	$5,000
Total Income for Period	**$22,500**
Less Advance Paid Previously	($20,000)
Due with This Accounting	$2,500

The publisher's terms of sale allow his customers to return books if those books do not sell. The normal contract will contain a sentence that allows the publisher to offset a "reasonable" reserve for returns against current sales. This means that the publisher has in his judgment reduced the actual sales he is reporting to you to protect himself against anticipated returns. To define "reasonable," the following sentence should be used:

> The publisher may, prior to payment of money to the author, deduct a reserve for anticipated returns of not more than 35% in the first two accounting periods and 20% thereafter.

Satisfactory Manuscript

Before the author can obtain any of the benefits under the contract, the manuscript must be *"completely satisfactory in form and content in the sole discretion of the publisher."* These are the magic words that are used in most publisher's contracts. The concept, now redefined, that the publisher had an unrestricted right to accept or reject a manuscript based upon his sole judgment, was first upheld by the courts in 1899 when, in the case of *Walker v. Edward Thompson*, the court said, "The work . . . is certainly as much a matter of taste as a suit of new clothes." For over three-quarters of a century, the courts permitted the publisher to reject manuscripts in his "sole discretion" without any reason other than his own "taste, fancy, or sensibility."

However, in 1982 a court held that the publisher could not reject a manuscript arbitrarily in "his sole discretion" but was held to a good faith standard. The case that changed the practice involved Senator Barry Goldwater, who wrote a book, *The Conscience of a Conservative*, with a coauthor. The authors repeatedly requested editorial assistance from Harcourt Brace, the publisher, and received none. When the completed manuscript was submitted, the editor at Harcourt relied on the traditional satisfactory manuscript language in the contract and rejected the book, saying in her view it was not satisfactory. The publisher believed, based on precedent, that they could reject the book and recover the $60,000 advance paid to Senator Goldwater. Not so.

The court held that the publisher in good faith had a duty to edit, to review the manuscript, point out areas to improve, and assist the author in making the book satisfactory. Harcourt had refused to edit, and the court allowed Senator Goldwater to keep the advance payment and to recover his manuscript. The court also noted in the decision that by the time the case was tried, this "unsatisfactory" manuscript had been edited by another publisher, accepted, published, and had become a best-seller. Courts will refuse to order a publisher to publish a book; however, if the rejections are in bad faith, courts now consistently allow the authors to retain their advance payments and also allow the author to sell the book to another publisher without any obligation to repay the advance.

Additional court decisions have set out a course of conduct that an author should follow to avoid any controversy over the satisfactory manuscript. The publisher should be provided with an outline of the book and such other material to be certain that the publisher and the author are agreed on the nature of the book. This outline should be referred to in the contract, for example:

> . . . the work, "The Merry Month of May," a novel of approximately 100,000 words substantially consistent with the outline attached . . .

Thereafter, the author should seek and use the editorial resources of the publisher, knowing that it is the publisher's duty to assist the author in improving the manuscript if possible. In some cases, the courts held that where the editor has reviewed and proposed changes to a portion of the manuscript, which the author completes in reliance on the editor's encouragement, the publisher may ultimately reject the book. However, in such cases, the author can keep the advance, retain the rights to the manuscript, and sell it to another publisher without repayment of the advance.

Reacting to such court decisions, publishers are now stating their willingness to help make the book better in the contract, but they retain the right to reject it if, after all the revisions, the book is still not satisfactory in their sole judgment. The progress made on behalf of authors is that they can keep their advance and sell the book to another publisher if the rejection is not in good faith. Most publishers will insist on the now outmoded phase *"completely satisfactory in form and content,"* but it is of no practical importance. Authors should not object to this phrase when it appears in the contract.

Subsidiary Rights

Most hardcover book publishers need the income generated from the sale of subsidiary rights (sales to paperback publishers, book clubs, etc.) to earn a profit for their publishing business as a whole. The hardcover publishing business is now and always has been a marginal business until the publisher develops a backlist (a list of previously published books that continue to sell with minimal expenses). Income from subsidiary rights is also crucial to the publisher, and the publisher will ask the author to allow him to exploit these rights. We listed the subsidiary rights on page 142. The rights being granted are described in the following pages.

Mass Market Paperback Rights

The most profitable subsidiary right for the author and publisher is the license for mass market paperback rights. The hardcover publisher will, at an appropriate time after publication, invite bids for the paperback rights. The paperback houses that bid offer a guaranteed nonrefundable sum payable as an advance against royalties. The sums paid for paperback rights for books by major authors may be substantial, many times exceeding one million dollars. When the royalties on sales exceed the one-million-dollar advance, the author and publisher receive additional payments. Books by first-time authors have also generated large advances for paperback rights. It is not unusual for the unheralded book that is well suited to the paperback format to generate bids of $100,000 or more. The advance and royalty received for subsidiary rights is normally shared equally by the publisher and the author. Keep in mind, however, that only about one in four hardcovers is later reprinted in mass market.

Book Club Rights

When there is a major book, one that a publisher believes will be a best-seller, book club rights are sometimes auctioned in the same manner as paperback rights. The hardcover publisher seeks a non-recoverable advance and royalty from the book club. Suitable but not spectacular books are often sold through direct negotiation between the hardcover publisher and the book club without an auction. Sums paid for major books are in the hundreds of thousands. Normally this income, too, is shared equally with the publisher.

Magazine Rights

Some books, especially timely books or celebrity books, lend themselves to serialization in magazines or newspapers either before publication (first serial rights) or after publication (second serial rights). Traditionally, the author receives a large share of the first serial rights (and often controls them), generally 85 to 90 percent. Normally, income from second serial rights is divided equally.

Audio and Video Rights

There are now tens of thousands of books recorded on audio and video cassettes and sold by audio publishers. These rights now represent a growing source of revenue. Most publishers will insist that they be allowed to license these rights. The author receives a share of the audio income, often 50 percent. Since some publishers are still not adept at selling these rights, the author is best served by allowing the publisher a reasonable chance, possibly two years, to sell the rights and then recovering them automatically if still unsold.

Foreign Rights

As described previously, the publisher often contracts with a publisher in the United Kingdom to sell an English-language book into this territory. Similarly, the publisher may license foreign translations of the work. As discussed previously, there should be a grant of these rights for a limited period of time with the right to recover them if no deals have been consummated that will result in publication within a reasonable period. The net income from licenses granted under this provision is usually 75 to 85 percent for the author, 25 to 15 percent for the publisher.

Rights Retained

Rarely, if ever, should an author grant movie, television, or dramatic rights. Publishers include these rights in their contracts, knowing a sophisticated author will strike them out. Publishers are not offended if these rights are excluded. With any remaining rights, the first-time author is best advised to be generous, but reserve the right to recover rights after a two- to three-year period if they are not exploited.

Early Payment

Money received by the publisher from the sales of subsidiary rights is included in the semiannual royalty statement. The royalty statement can come as much as nine months after receipt of the money by the hardcover publisher. It is not fair for the publisher to retain the author's share of this money for extended periods. In some instances, the publisher will accept an addition to his standard contract as follows:

Notwithstanding anything to the contrary herein, the publisher will pay the author any money received for subsidiary rights sixty days after receipt providing the advance paid to the author has been earned.

Hardcover-Softcover Deals

Many of the major paperback publishers also publish hardcover books. It is becoming common for these publishers to buy hardcover, trade, and mass market paperback rights. The publisher pays one single advance, sets the royalty rate for each edition, and normally commits to publish in all three formats in sequence, or if he does not, he allows the unexploited right to revert to the author. The publisher prefers this because it is less expensive to buy all rights together even if he pays a somewhat larger advance than he would pay for hardcover-only rights. The author often prefers this because the money paid for all three rights is greater and she receives 100 percent of the royalties. Under a hard-soft deal, 100 percent of the royalties on the paperback are received by the author. In a hardcover-only deal, the hardcover publisher sells rights to a third party for a paperback edition, and the publisher and the author share the income equally. Authors who believe that the paperback income is likely to be greater than hardcover income accept hardcover-softcover deals.

Approvals

The publisher and the author are inextricably tied together in a joint enterprise to make the book successful. While many publishers may be reluctant to involve the first-time author in the publishing process, the author should have the prior right of approval for any contract entered into for a subsidiary right, for the cover and interior design, for advertising and promotion pieces printed to promote the book. (Admittedly, it is difficult for a novice author to secure such approval; what might be agreed upon alternatively is "consultation," wherein the author is consulted on such points and at least can give her two cents' worth.) The author should also have the right to approve in advance the sale or transfer of her contract to a third party. Unilateral action by a publisher may seem to be expeditious. However, involving the author creates a positive atmosphere leading to a long-term relationship.

Commitments on Marketing and Advertising

Every book receives marketing at the publisher's expense. Marketing might include catalogs, posters, exposure at conventions, mailings, etc. The publisher might also spend money on advertising and promotion in the form of print, radio, or television ads as well as author tours.

Unless the author is a major writer, the publisher will rarely include a specific commitment in the contract as to the amount of advertising or marketing money to be spent promoting the book. However, sometimes the publisher will write a side letter to the author setting forth the advertising and marketing planned and the money expected to be spent. Unless it is a book that the publisher believes can be made into a best-seller, the amount of advertising dollars to be committed is small—normally one dollar a book (or less) based upon the initial printing. Thus, if the initial printing is ten thousand copies the entire ad budget is ten thousand dollars. Publishers depend largely on "free advertising"—reviews and author exposure on television and radio.

Warranty and Indemnification

Since the publisher relies on the author to prepare an original work and keep the text free from libel or invasion of privacy, the publisher will ask the author to warrant that the work is her own, is libel free, and that she has not invaded the privacy of any individual. The publisher asks the author to indemnify him in the event of a claim or suit for infringement of copyright, libel, or invasion of privacy. There is almost no way for the author to avoid this warranty and indemnification. However, the author should ask that the publisher's libel insurance policy be used to cover her liability in the event an action is brought. The author can also ask to have the amount for which she is responsible not exceed the amount of the advance payment she receives.

Timeliness

As a part of the contract, the author promises to deliver her manuscript on a certain date. The publisher must commit to publish, usually twelve to eighteen months after receipt of a "satisfactory manuscript." The stricter contracts will state that "time is of the essence." This is a warning that timeliness is a precise obligation and failure to deliver on time will be a breach of the contract. This provision applies to delivery dates when the book is related to a time-sensitive event. For example, a book that is to be used in connection with a scheduled art exhibition must be delivered on the date promised. Failure to adhere to this date may allow the injured party to terminate the contract and sue for damages. Absent these circumstances, dates of delivery for manuscript and dates of publication can be extended and the contract amended in writing accordingly. Publishers are generally amenable to reasonable delays if they know about them far enough in advance.

Exclusivity and Option

Publishers usually ask for a one- or two-year period during which the author will not write a book that will be directly competitive to the work covered by the contract. If this is a burdensome provision, an effort should be made to omit it or limit the scope of the exclusivity. For example, a professor who writes regularly on the same subject for professional reasons must seek an exception that will allow her to be productive. (While the author may be bound, notably the courts have held that *publishers* may publish competitive books as long as they continue to use their best efforts to promote the author's book.)

The publisher may also ask for an option on the author's next book. The publisher feels he should have the first opportunity to acquire the next book written by the author before it is offered to another publisher. In arguing for this option, the publisher points to the effort and expense he will undertake in the book to be published. Authors should avoid making such a commitment, especially without having experienced the publisher's efforts on behalf of the book currently under contract. However, the clause can often be reduced to a first look at the manuscript, or detailed outline and sample chapter. Unless the parties agree to the terms, the author retains the right to take the book to another publisher—with no strings attached such as an option to match the highest bidder.

In Print and Termination

The author has a right to require the publisher to keep the book in print in a sufficient quantity to satisfy reasonable demand from potential readers. The standard provision obligates the publisher to do this. If he does not, the author may terminate the contract. Some contracts allow the author to purchase the materials that will enable her to reprint the book on her own at a favorable price, or allow another publisher to use these materials. Since it is now possible by use of Print-on-Demand technology to print in very small quantities, it is important for the author to require a minimum unit sale so that the parties understand what is meant by "in print."

Remedy

It is in the author's interest to have arbitration as a remedy in the event of a dispute that cannot be resolved by direct negotiation. Publishers will insist on using the courts to resolve differences, knowing the author has limited resources and legal expenses would be prohibitive. Publishers usually resist, but the author should negotiate for an arbitration provision.

Summary

You are now contract literate. This does not make you a lawyer, but it will make you a better-informed client. You should have a grasp of the rationale underlying a publishing contract, the terms used, the rules of the road, and what the normal commercial practices are, especially in terms of money you might expect from a publisher.

Your education continues when we review an actual contract and discuss it in the pages of Chapter 10. It is important that before you are asked to sign a contract, you have studied the terms of a typical contract. In some instances, material we have just discussed may be repeated and amplified to improve your contract literacy. Chapters 8, 9, and 10 should be read together. This should take some of the mystery out of the contract you will, it is hoped, be asked to sign.

10

The Contract Reality Check

Having completed your short course in contract literacy and negotiated the business terms of your contract, you are ready for the *real* contract—a daunting document.

Most publishers refuse to make their author-publisher contracts available for publication. Even The Authors Guild (which should be on the side of all unpublished authors) refuses permission to reprint their contract, one with excellent explanatory advice that would make any publisher's contract more equitable to the author. Access to that contract is a member benefit, and available only to those who join The Authors Guild. However, The Authors Guild Web site, www.authorsguild.org, does offer some basic contract tips.

With limited access to actual contracts, you should seek the counsel of a lawyer familiar with drafting and reviewing publishing contracts. In addition, it is important that you see an entire publishing contract, study the terms on your own, and ask your attorney and editor to explain issues that may be troublesome or confusing. To introduce you to what you are likely to see, I have created a sample standard contract. While every publisher's contract will be different, the contract shown here is typical.

I have written this chapter as a conversation between you, the author (A), and your lawyer (L) to provide a feel for the process used to review and discuss a contract.

ABC PUBLISHING

AGREEMENT, made this ____ day of _____, 20____, by and between ABC Publishing, Inc., a New York corporation, having its offices at Pumpkin Ridge Road, Rye, New York 10580, hereinafter referred to as "ABC," and Mary K. Smith, hereinafter referred to as "Author."

WITNESSETH

WHEREAS, the Author has agreed to deliver to ABC a manuscript tentatively entitled, "HOW TO SUCCEED IN PUBLISHING" (the "Work"); and

WHEREAS, ABC agrees to publish or to arrange for publication of the Work and any revisions thereof, on the terms and conditions specified below.

NOW, THEREFORE, in consideration of the promises and covenants contained herein, the parties agree as follows:

A: This looks straightforward. Would you change this?

L: Yes, I would. As you recall, in order to provide a baseline to determine whether the manuscript, as finally submitted, is what you and the publisher had in mind at the time the contract was signed, it is advisable to describe *How to Succeed in Publishing* by adding *"a nonfiction work of approximately 100,000 words consistent with the outline attached to the contract."* Should there be a dispute concerning whether or not the manuscript is satisfactory, this description provides the basis to determine the understanding of the parties at the time.

Because of the size of most conglomerates, many publishers have a series of imprints. Random House is an excellent example. In the same building bearing the name of Random House, you will find Villard, Knopf, and Pantheon, all trade houses with their own editors, support personnel, and areas of expertise. The imprint used may determine the care and attention your book will receive. Since this is the time to get these issues clarified, it is useful to identify the publishing imprint to be used when the book is published. If the manuscript is to be published by XYZ, a subsidiary or division of

ABC, the party should be identified as "XYZ, a subsidiary of ABC" or "XYZ, a division of ABC."

1. Grant of Rights.

(a) The Author hereby grants and assigns to ABC, its licenses and assigns for the full term of copyright available in each country included within the territory covered by this Agreement under any copyright laws now or hereinafter in force:

(i) the exclusive right to print, publish, distribute, and sell ("publish") in all languages in book form throughout the world and to license others to do so, a work now entitled HOW TO SUCCEED IN PUBLISHING;

(ii) The additional and subsidiary rights in the Work hereinafter set forth in 6 below;

(b) All rights to the Work not granted to ABC by this agreement shall remain the property of the Author.

A: This Grant of Rights clause is one I think I would discuss and try to get changed. It seems to me that I may not have any rights left. When I grant the right to "print, publish, and sell in all languages in book form" this means hardcover, trade paperback, and mass market paperback—everything.

L: You're absolutely right.

A: And when they add "in all languages," I'm granting English and all translation rights.

L: Correct again.

A: As I read this, I have granted them world rights on everything including subsidiary rights. If you add to this the phrase "for the full term of the copyright" it appears that this is an all-encompassing grant of rights forever.

L: All encompassing, yes; forever, no. You have the right to terminate the contract and recover the rights after thirty-five years. Nevertheless, this is a broad grant of rights.

A: What can I do to attempt to retain some rights?

L: Unless you are an important author, there is very little you
   can do. There are some openings in later paragraphs to ask
   for a reversion of rights if the publisher does not use them
   after a reasonable period. We will discuss these opportunities as we get to applicable paragraphs in the contract.

2. The Manuscript

(a) At the Author's own expense, she agrees to deliver to ABC on or
before August 1, 2002, one copy of the manuscript and computer disks compatible with the publisher's computerized system suitable for a book of
100,000 words in length, satisfactory in form and content to ABC. The Author
further agrees to furnish photographs, drawings, charts, illustrations, index,
appendix, bibliography, and any other related materials (the "Related Materials") along with any written authorization by all third-party proprietors of
copyrighted text and illustrative material contained in the Work and the
proper forms of copyright notice for such material. (If the Author fails to
obtain such permissions or provide such notices, ABC may do so and charge
the cost to the Author.) All Related Materials will be in form and content satisfactory to ABC. If the Author fails to deliver any of the Related Materials or
if the Related Materials are not in form and content satisfactory to ABC, ABC
may obtain, create, or revise such missing or unsatisfactory materials and
charge the reasonable cost thereof to the author. If retyping or reformatting
the manuscript is necessary to make it ready for press, ABC may have it
retyped and charge the cost of such retyping to the Author.

(b) If the Author does not deliver a completed manuscript to ABC by the
agreed-upon date, or ABC, in its sole discretion, deems the manuscript to be
unsatisfactory in either form or content, then ABC may, at any time thereafter, serve a written notice upon him/her requiring him/her to deliver a complete and satisfactory manuscript. If the Author does not deliver a completed
manuscript within thirty (30) days of the giving of notice or does not deliver
a revised satisfactory manuscript within ninety (90) days of the giving of
notice, ABC may terminate this Agreement at any time by written notice to
the Author specifying the date of termination. If a termination notice is
served, all amounts advanced by ABC to the Author pursuant to this Agreement shall be repaid to ABC by him/her and the Agreement will terminate as
of the date specified in the notice. However, ABC may cancel its notice of termination any time before its effective date by simultaneously giving notice
of its decision to cancel and returning to the Author any portion of the
advance repaid by the Author pursuant to the preceding sentence.

A: What should I watch out for here?

L: This is a crucial paragraph. Let's discuss each element. First, the delivery date. You are committing to deliver the manuscript by August 1, 2002. The date can be changed by mutual agreement and most publishers will grant a delay. If you contemplate missing the deadline, be sure to get a written amendment to the contract. While the courts have ruled that whenever authors miss the deadline by a "reasonable" length of time, the publisher cannot terminate the contract, there is no need to leave yourself open to a cancellation of the contract, when most publishers will grant a reasonable delay.

You have agreed to furnish a disk and one hard copy. Be sure you will be able to provide the manuscript in a compatible software format. Ask the publisher to add specific words, such as "Word 2000," if this is what he has in mind.

You have also obligated yourself to provide, at your expense, all the illustrative materials, copyright notices, and permissions. If your book is heavily illustrated, you may be incurring considerable expense. Sometimes the publisher will share these expenses. Make sure you know the amount of potential expense, consider this carefully, and negotiate for cost sharing now.

Note that if you do not meet these obligations to the publisher's satisfaction, the publisher may obtain the materials and permission and/or reformat your manuscript to comply with his software, and charge this to you. The publisher may owe you additional payments, and these amounts could be deducted from money otherwise due to you. You should set a maximum amount that can be charged to the author.

Section (b) contains a very important concept. The phrase to be studied is, "If . . . ABC, in its sole discretion, deems the manuscript to be unsatisfactory in form and content . . . ABC may terminate the agreements . . . and all amounts advanced to the author shall be repaid to ABC." The courts have ruled that any such rejection of a manuscript must be in good faith and have, in their decisions, set standards to determine the publisher's good faith. This does not concern me because the words in the contract must be read with the implied condition of good faith.

However, I would try to have the publisher agree that if he rejects the manuscript, the moneys to be repaid can come from the "first proceeds" received on a subsequent sale of the book. This means that if the publisher rejects the book, the author may sell it to another publisher and repay the advance when he receives payment from the new publisher. Many publishers have specific language they use for this, and will amend the contract accordingly. Most publishers understand, realistically, that most first-time authors will have already spent the advance they received and do not have sufficient personal resources to repay the money before they sell the book to another publisher. Sometimes the publisher may only give you a year to find a new publisher, after which the publisher will require the author to repay the advance out of her own resources. If, however, you can get a "first proceeds" clause, and you probably can, it is worth the time it will take you to negotiate this change in the contract.

3. Proofs.

(a) The Author shall read and correct his/her proofs and return them to ABC within [insert number] days of the proofs having been sent to the Author. Should the Author fail to return the corrected proofs within the allotted time period, ABC may publish the Work as printed with any changes or corrections as ABC deems necessary. All costs of the corrections and alterations in proofs (other than printer's errors) in excess of ten percent (10%) of the original cost of the composition shall be deducted by ABC from any sums due and owing to the Author.

A: This seems fair.

L: It is. You are on notice to correct proofs promptly and to be thorough. And this clause informs you it is too late and costly to make many corrections after the printer's proof.

4. Agreement to Publish.

(a) ABC agrees to publish the Work at its own expense within eighteen (18) months after acceptance of the final manuscript, except that this publication date will be extended to the extent reasonable and necessary in case of a delay caused by any circumstances beyond ABC's control, including, but not limited to, strikes, fires, shortages of labor or materials, mechanical difficulties, governmental restrictions, and acts of God. ABC has the sole discretion to decide the Work's format, style of printing and binding, cover presentation, trademark, logo, imprint or other identification, retail price, and terms of sale, distribution, advertising, and promotion.

(b) If the Work is not published within the time period specified above, including any allowance for an extension due to circumstances beyond ABC's control, the Author may terminate this agreement by written notice which shall become effective six (6) months after receipt by ABC unless the Work is published before the expiration of the period. Upon such termination all rights granted hereunder will revert to the Author. Any payments already made to the Author under this Agreement in advances shall be his/hers to keep and the retaining of such advances shall be deemed to fully discharge all of ABC's obligations to the Author. No other damages, claims, actions, or proceedings, legal or equitable, founded on breach of contract, default, or failure to publish may be pursued against ABC by the Author or his/her agents, heirs, or assigns.

(c) In no event shall ABC be obligated to publish or have any liability to the Author for failure to publish (or any related cause of action) the Work when either the Author or ABC has been given notice of a claim, demand, or suit alleging that the Work (i) infringes the copyright or violates the right of privacy or any other right of third parties, (ii) contains libelous or obscene matter, or (iii) when the Author is unable or unwilling to verify statements in the Work purporting to be truthful or factual.

(d) ABC will not be obligated to publish the Work if ABC's legal counsel is of the opinion that it contains unlawful material or material which may violate the rights of any person. If, in ABC's opinion, there appears to be a substantial risk of legal action or liability on account of the Work, the Author will make any necessary revisions or deletions to remove any such risk. If the Author does not make or authorize ABC to make the necessary revisions or deletions or if the Work is unpublishable in the opinion of ABC's legal counsel, then ABC may terminate this agreement in writing any time prior to publication. In the event of such a termination, any and all amounts advanced to the Author by ABC pursuant to this agreement shall be promptly repaid by the Author.

A: Let me see if I understand this. The publisher agrees to publish eighteen months after he accepts the manuscript, unless there are circumstances beyond his control. Is this reasonable?

L: Yes, it is. However, I would not accept an obligation to publish in twenty-four months, which you may find in some contracts. Twenty-four months is really too long unless it is a long and very difficult book to print. Some art books may require an extended period.

A: Then, if he does not publish in time or, I guess, a reasonable time after that date, which is defined as six months, I am allowed to keep the advance payments and my manuscript, which I can sell to another publisher.

L: That is correct. If the publisher fails to publish, your only remedy is to be able to keep the advance payment and the rights to your book. You cannot sue the publisher for any income you might have lost by his failure to perform under the contract.

A: Let me say this once more. I have a manuscript that is satisfactory to the publisher. He fails to publish in eighteen months. I wait six more months and then notify him that I am terminating the contract. I have lost all this time when there may have been another publisher ready to publish my book, and I cannot sue for damages.

L: As they say in *My Fair Lady*, I think you've got it. However, in a real world, you monitor the publisher's progress. After you submit the manuscript, you should receive some evidence of the book appearing in the publisher's next catalog. If there are no signs of activity, you should initiate a discussion that should allow you to terminate the contract according to the provision in the contract. This requires a new negotiation, but it is in the interests of both the publisher and the author to resolve this amicably.

A: I have no problem with the publisher refusing to publish if my book may violate the law.

L: Nor should you, as long as the determination by the publisher is based on a legal opinion.

5. Royalties and Advances.

(a) ABC shall pay to the Author royalties on sales, less returns, of copies of ABC's editions of the Work as follows:

(1) on all hardcover copies sold through ordinary channels of trade in the United States (except as otherwise provided below), the following percentages of the suggested retail price:

      (a) 1–5,000 copies: 10%

      (b) 5,000–10,000 copies: $12^{1}/_{2}$%

      (c) in excess of 10,000 copies: 15%

(2) on all hardcover copies sold in the United States at discounts higher than ABC's announced discounts for wholesale and retail accounts in the book trade and (i) on a nonrefundable basis; or (ii) as special sales, as premiums, to catalog accounts, to book fairs, or outside the ordinary channels of the book trade, 10% of the amount received by ABC;

(3) on all hardcover copies sold outside the United States or for export to Canada or to other countries throughout the territory, 10% of the amounts received by ABC;

(4) on all paperback copies sold through ordinary channels of trade in the United States (except as otherwise provided below), $7^{1}/_{2}$% of the suggested retail price;

(5) on all paperback copies sold in the United States at discounts higher than ABC's announced discounts for wholesale and retail accounts in the book trade and (i) on a nonrefundable basis; or (ii) as special sales, as premiums, to catalog accounts, to book fairs, or outside of the ordinary channels of the book trade, $7^{1}/_{2}$% of the amounts received by ABC;

(6) on all paperback copies sold outside the United States or for export to Canada or to other countries throughout the Territory, $7^{1}/_{2}$% of the amounts received by ABC;

(7) on all large print copies sold through ordinary channels of trade in the United States (except as otherwise provided below), 10% of the suggested retail price;

(8) on all large print copies sold in the United States at discounts higher than ABC's announced discounts for wholesale and retail accounts in the book trade and (i) on a nonrefundable basis; or (ii) as special sales, as premiums, to catalog accounts, to book fairs, or outside of the ordinary channels of the book trade, 10% of the amounts received by ABC;

(9) on all large print copies sold outside the United States or for export to Canada or to other countries throughout the Territory, 10% of the amounts received by ABC;

(10) on all copies of ABC's editions of the Work sold directly by ABC to consumers in response to mail order or other direct-response solicitations sponsored by ABC, 5% of the price paid by the consumer, exclusive of shipping and handling charges;

(11) on all copies of ABC's edition of the Work sold as remainders at more than the cost of manufacture, 10% of the amounts received by ABC (ABC shall use its best efforts to give the Author notice of ABC's intention to remainder copies of the Work; ABC shall offer the Author 25 free copies of the Work, and give the Author a reasonable opportunity to purchase additional copies at ABC's manufacturing cost; however, ABC's failure to do so shall not be considered a breach of this Agreement nor give the Author any claim for damages);

(12) on copies given to or sold to the Author, given away to promote sales or to charitable institutions, sold at or below the cost of manufacture or damaged or destroyed, no royalties shall be paid.

(b) Only copies sold under 5(a)(1) shall be counted in determining the royalty escalations described in 5(a)(1).

(c) As an advance against all royalties and all proceeds from the disposition of subsidiary rights due the Author under this Agreement, ABC shall pay to the Author the sum of $20,000.00 payable:

(1) $10,000.00 upon execution of this Agreement;

(2) $10,000.00 upon ABC's acceptance for publication of the complete and final manuscript for the Work.

A: I admit I'm confused. I do understand paragraphs (a)(1) and (a)(4) because the royalty rate is one on which we agreed, and paragraphs (c)(1) and (c)(2) because this is the advance we agreed upon. But what about these other paragraphs, which seem to be reducing the rates of royalty for special situations? What is this all about?

L: It is confusing because there are so many exceptions. Basically publishers, by practice over the years, asked the author to give up some of her royalty payment if ABC must sell into a difficult market or if the publisher's income is reduced. The principle is sound, but the application of the principle places a disproportionate economic burden on the author's shoulders. Consider the case under (a)(2) when ABC sells at "higher than Publisher's announced discounts" the author receives "10% of the amount received by ABC."

What this means is that if ABC sells a book with a retail price of $15 at the regular discount, the net received by ABC is $8.25 and the author's royalty at 15 percent is $2.25. If ABC, in order to make a large sale, increases his discount to 60 percent, on the same $15 retail book he would get $6 from his customer rather than $8.25 and the author gets 10 percent of the amount received, or 60 cents, as compared to $2.25 for a sale made at the full retail price. The publisher loses $2.25 in income; the author loses $1.65. By reducing the author's income, the publisher comes closer than the author to retaining its income.

Some publishers have changed this paragraph on their own, by reducing the royalty to the author in proportion to the loss of receipts by the publisher. Obviously, both the publisher and the author benefit when large sales are made, even at lower prices. And it is reasonable to seek to share the lost income, but to saddle the author with a disproportionate burden is believed by many, including The Authors Guild, to be unfair.

When you see this provision in a contract, you should do the arithmetic with the publisher and make an effort to get the percentage changed, but it should not be a deal breaker for you. Become a best-selling author and the publisher might modify this provision in the next contract. The object of this negotiation is to get a contract, even though there are some clauses that may appear to be unfair.

6. Grant of Subsidiary Rights.

(a) The Author grants all rights as defined below to ABC throughout the world in all languages for the life of the copyright, whether such rights are exercised in whole or in part.

(b) Definitions. The following phrases shall have the following meanings when used in this Agreement:

(i) "Selection Rights" shall mean the right to use material from the work in the English language in abridged, adapted, and condensed versions in book form, on the radio, and in anthologies and other compilations in book form;

(ii) "First Serial Rights" shall mean the right to use material from the Work in the English language in newspapers, magazines, and other periodicals including abridged, adapted, and condensed versions, whether in one or more parts (before publication in book form);

(iii) "Second Serial Rights" shall mean the right to use material from the Work in the English language in newspapers, magazines, and other periodicals including abridged, adapted, and condensed versions, whether in one or more parts (after publication in book form);

(iv) "Microfilm Rights" shall mean the right to use material from the Work on microfilm or microfiche and in information storage and retrieval systems or in connection with teaching machines, whether in machine or human languages;

(v) "Print Rights" shall mean Selection Rights, First Serial Rights, Second Serial Rights, and Microfilm Rights;

(vi) "Dramatic Rights" shall mean theatrical presentation rights, motion picture rights, television rights (including cassettes and other devices for home play), and any other similar mechanical or electronic visual reproduction rights including film strips, and any other method now known or hereinafter devised;

(vii) "Audio Rights" shall mean mechanical and electronical (other than radio) sound reproduction rights (including records, tape recordings, sound cassettes, and other methods now known or hereinafter devised);

(viii) "Merchandising Rights" shall mean the sale of rights for use in merchandise such as "T-shirts," etc.;

(ix) "Translation Rights" shall mean the translation from the English language to a foreign language;

(x) "Electronic Rights" shall mean recording or storage retrieval of text and illustrations by electronic or other means, the result of which serves as a substitute for the sale of a book, such as a book delivered on line or an electronic book;

(c) All rights in the Work not granted to ABC by this Agreement shall remain the Property of the Author.

A: If I sign this, it means I will grant all subsidiary rights for the life of the copyright to the publisher.

L: That is correct. There are a few major changes that should be made. First, I suggest you delete "Dramatic Rights" and "Merchandising Rights." Customarily, an author retains these rights, because she probably will be able to get an agent who specializes in the sale of these rights to represent her once the book is published, especially if it is successful. Very few publishers have departments expert in selling these rights. As a consequence, they usually will relinquish them. Publishers of children's books who are familiar with licensing book characters often insist on retaining merchandising rights and should be allowed to do this for a limited period, probably two years. If the publisher has not exploited this right at the end of that time, it should revert to you. If, however, the publisher can demonstrate his ability to sell these rights, you may wish to give him the first opportunity to do this.

The publisher is normally well equipped to sell rights such as mass market paperback, book clubs, etc. However, I recommend that you negotiate a time frame during which they can sell these rights, say two to three years; if licenses have not been entered into by then, these rights would revert to you for your exploitation. This gives the publisher a fair opportunity, and then allows you to pursue this sale of the rights with an agent on your own. The grant of electronic rights should be made subject to the author's prior approval. Online distribution of books and publication of e-books is in the early stages of development. The author should have the right to review each deal prior to the publisher making a deal.

7. Share of Receipts of Subsidiary Rights.

The amount received by ABC from the following rights shall be shared by the Author and ABC in the percentages indicated below.

		Author	ABC
(i)	Reprint Rights to Work in the English language in book form except by book clubs or like organizations	50%	50%
(ii)	Book Club Rights to the Work in the English Language in book form (whether full-length, abridged, condensed, or adapted versions)	50%	50%
(iii)	Selection Rights, except to book clubs or like organizations	50%	50%
(iv)	First Serial Rights	90%	10%
(v)	Second Serial Rights	50%	50%
(vi)	Microfilm Rights	50%	50%
(vii)	English Language Licenses in U.K.	80%	20%
(viii)	Translations in all languages	75%	25%
(ix)	Audio Recordings	75%	25%
(x)	Dramatic Rights*	75%	25%
(xi)	Movie and Television Rights*	75%	25%
(xii)	Merchandising Rights*	75%	25%
(xiii)	Electronic Rights	50%	50%

*Assuming these rights remain in the grant to the publisher; if not, strike through these items or any items excluded from the grant of rights.

A: All these splits look about right.

L: These subrights splits are very standard and acceptable. The battle over the equitable division of electronic rights is still being waged, but if this publisher is making a major investment in developing electronic rights, he deserves an opportunity to exploit these rights.

8. Royalty Statements and Payments.

(a) ABC shall prepare semiannual statements accounting for all payments due the Author under this Agreement. ABC shall send each such statement to the Author within ninety (90) days after the close of each period (January 31 and July 31 of each year) accompanied by payment to the Author of the amounts due to him/her for that period. If payment is not timely made, the Author may demand in writing that payment be made within forty-five (45) days. If ABC fails to comply, the Author may immediately terminate this Agreement and all rights shall revert to him/her.

(b) Each royalty statement shall report for each edition of the Work the number of copies sold (including total sales to date), the list price, the royalty rate, amount of royalties, the amount of reserve withheld for returns, and the gross amount received pursuant to each license, if applicable, granted by ABC. With each royalty statement, ABC shall send the author copies of statements received by ABC from its licensees during the accounting period.

(c) Upon written request by the Author, he/she or his/her designated representative may examine, during normal business hours, the books and records of ABC insofar as they relate to the Work. If such examination discloses an error of five percent (5%) or more with respect to any royalty statement, ABC shall reimburse the Author for his/her costs of the examination; otherwise such costs shall be borne by the Author.

A: This looks straightforward. Is there anything that I should be concerned with in this paragraph?

L: You're right—it's a standard paragraph used by most publishers. The key issue here is the "reserve for returns" provision. It is a sad truth that booksellers and wholesalers return large quantities of books to publishers at their discretion, and publishers appropriately retain a sufficient amount of money to cover any possible overpayment of royalties to the author. How large a return is reasonable? You should try to have the publisher insert the phrase "up to 35% during the first year of sale and 20% thereafter." The rationale for this provision is that the returns are larger in the first year, and when a more consistent rate of sale is established the bookseller will order to meet his expected sales and have fewer returns. If you fail to convince the publisher to revise the language, relax; you can be assured that the worst result is that the royalties due to you in one period will arrive in the next period, a delay of six months.

A far more important issue is the payment of large sums that may be received between royalty statements. If you are fortunate enough to have your book achieve substantial subsidiary rights sales, significant sums ($100,000 or more) paid by a licensee could be held by your publisher for what might be up to nine months, depriving you of the use of your share of the money. You should be able to have the publisher insert a phrase that would require payments to you within thirty days after receipt of $100,000 or more, as long as the advance payment made to you has been earned. If it is unearned, the publisher can retain a sum sufficient to recover the unearned advance before he pays your share.

9. Copyright.

(a) The copyright in the Work shall belong to the Author. ABC shall, within three (3) months of first publication, duly register a claim for a United States Copyright in the Work, in the name of the Author as "claimant." ABC shall print in every copy of the Work a copyright notice required by United States copyright law and the Universal Copyright Convention. Every license granted by ABC hereunder to reproduce and distribute copies of the Work shall contain a condition requiring the licensee to print the aforesaid copyright notice in all copies.

(b) If the copyright in the Work is infringed by a third party, whichever party to this Agreement first learns of the infringement will inform the other. Author will have the right to join ABC in bringing suit against the alleged infringer. If the Author decides to do so, he/she will share equally in the expenses of the action and in any sums recovered as a result. Neither the Author nor ABC will be required to bring suit. Should one party decline to participate in a suit, the other party may proceed, bearing all expenses and retaining all sums recovered.

A: This looks routine.

L: There is the issue of the name in which the copyright is registered. Since the Author is the owner of the work, it should be registered in her name. You should make a note to check at the end of three months to be certain the copyright registration has been filed. Under the current U.S. copyright law, there is no requirement for registration, but there are significant benefits to the author and publisher from filing, should there be an infringement.

10. Warranty and Indemnification.

(a) The author hereby covenants and represents:

(i) that he/she is the sole author of the Work (may use title of the Work in place of "Work") and is the sole owner of the rights herein granted and that he/she has not assigned, pledged, or encumbered such rights or entered into any agreement which would derogate or conflict with the rights granted to the publisher ("ABC") herein and will not do any of the above;

(ii) that he/she has the full right, power, and authority to enter into this Agreement and to grant the rights herein granted;

(iii) that except for materials of others, permission for use of which has or will be obtained by her/him, the Work is original, previously unpublished, and neither the Work nor any material portion hereof is in the public domain;

(iv) that the Work does not contain any material which violates any right of privacy, which is libelous, or which violates any personal or other right of any kind of any person or entity;

(v) that the Work contains no material which would violate any contract of hers/his, express or implied, or which would disclose any information given to him/her on the understanding that it would not be published or disclosed;

(vi) that no material in the Work plagiarizes or pirates any other work or infringes on any copyright, trademark, or other proprietary right; and

(vii) that no recipe, formula, or instruction contained in the Work is injurious to the user or others [used only if applicable].

(b) The Author shall indemnify and hold harmless ABC, its officers, directors, employees, and agents from any loss, liability (including settlements entered into in good faith), cost, damage, payment, or other expense (including reasonable attorneys' fees and disbursements) paid or incurred in connection with any claim, demand, recovery, suit, civil or criminal proceeding arising out of the breach or alleged breach of any of the foregoing warranties and representations.

(c) Upon the receipt of any notice of any claim, demand, recovery, suit, civil or criminal proceedings which alleges facts inconsistent with the foregoing representations and warranties, ABC shall have the right to withhold any sums payable to the Author in reasonable amounts as security for the payment of his/her possible obligations pursuant to the indemnity contained in subparagraph (b) above. It is the intention of the parties that the right herein granted shall not be unreasonably or frivolously exercised by ABC.

A: What does this mean, really?

L: One of the main purposes of a contract, and one reason why the contract is so lengthy, is to anticipate future problems. Over the years, some authors have borrowed too freely from other copyrighted works, or they have based characters in a novel too closely on living persons and described these individuals in a way that might identify the individual and negatively affect the public's perception of the individual's character. The publisher has no way of knowing upon what sources the author has relied. As a result, he is putting you on notice in this provision that if you have infringed on a copyright or libeled an individual, you will be held financially responsible for these acts.

A: This could be thousands of dollars in damages and lawyers' fees.

L: True, but the remedy for this is to avoid copyright infringement and libel. Nevertheless, you should ask the publisher to cover you with his liability insurance if he has such a policy, limited to your advance—another change in the contract many publishers accept.

11. <u>Noncompetition.</u>

The Author shall not permit or arrange for the publication, distribution, or sale in the Territory [defined in the Grant of Rights provision] other than by ABC, of any work which will compete with the Work or diminish the value of any subsidiary or additional rights granted by this Agreement except that the Author may grant licenses for the exploitation of any rights reserved to the Author under this Agreement.

A: I understand the need not to interfere with the publisher's ability to sell my current book by writing a competitive book, but suppose I still have to earn a living?

L: Your point is well taken. You should try to limit the time by adding "during the two years following publication." Add the phrase "directly competitive with the Work and likely to diminish its sale" or seek to exclude books or articles required in pursuit of an academic requirement or writing in connection with your profession. You might mention to the publisher that he has the right, established by courts, to publish a book that might compete with *your* book as long as he continues to use his best efforts in selling your book. If he can compete, it might be reasonable to allow you to write another book as long as the book is not "*directly* competitive."

12. <u>Option.</u>

The author agrees to negotiate with ABC in good faith the same exclusive rights contained herein in his/her next written book-length work whether written under Author's real name or under any pseudonym ("Next Work") and shall submit an outline or the completed manuscript to ABC before offering such rights to any other publisher directly or indirectly. ABC shall have thirty (30) days after receipt of the submission within which to notify the Author of whether it will exercise its option with respect to the Next Work. If ABC notifies the Author of its desire to exercise such option within the permitted time period, the Author and ABC shall negotiate the terms of an agreement for a period of sixty (60) days commencing upon the end of the thirty (30) day period described in the preceding sentence. If a mutually satisfactory agreement is not reached at the end of sixty (60) days, the

Author shall be free to offer said rights; provided, however, that the Author shall not enter into an agreement for the publication of his/her Next Work with any other publisher (i) upon the same terms or terms less favorable to the Author than those offered by ABC or (ii) upon terms more favorable to the Author than those offered by ABC without first giving ABC a further option to enter into an agreement as favorable. Such further option shall be exercised by giving notice to the Author within thirty (30) days of ABC's receipt of the Author's written notice of that offer.

A: The reason for the option clause is that it is in the interest of the author and the publisher to build a long-term relationship. It often requires more than one book to establish a dedicated readership. The publisher is more likely to invest if he has a chance to acquire subsequent books. Nevertheless, this option clause concerns me. What if the publisher has not promoted my book or I cannot get along with the editor? Why should I be bound to this provision?

L: You should not. Most authors, and The Authors Guild, agree with you. If the publisher has not performed in a satisfactory manner, it is fair that you have the opportunity to seek a new publisher without giving your current publisher the opportunity to match a competitive offer. It is very difficult to get a competitive publisher to give you an offer on your next book knowing that your original publisher can buy the book by simply meeting his offer. As indicated, the publisher defends this provision by saying, "We like to keep our authors and we know each succeeding book is helped by the previous book." The compromise in language most acceptable to publishers and authors is to give the original publisher sixty days to make an offer, and eliminate the obligation to reveal any competitive offers, enabling you to accept the best offer. If possible, the option provision should be omitted. A happy author will stay with a good publisher because it makes good economic and professional sense to do so.

13. <u>Out of Print.</u>

(a) After receipt by ABC of a written notice, the Author may terminate this Agreement (provided, however, he/she is not in default or breach of the Agreement) if

     (i) after five (5) years from the Work's initial publication date, all editions, whether hardcover or paperback, of the Work, go out of print; and

     (ii) ABC fails to reprint or cause a licensee to reprint a U.S. edition within twelve (12) months after receipt of the Author's written demand. It is understood and agreed that ABC shall notify the Author within six (6) months of such demand of its intention to reprint or revert the Work. The notice to terminate shall become effective thirty (30) days after receipt thereof by ABC. All rights granted hereunder, except the right to dispose of existing stock, shall revert to the Author and ABC has no further obligation or liability to the Author except for his/her share of earnings to be paid when and as due. If ABC (or its licensee) shall have been prevented from reprinting by circumstances beyond its control including, but not limited to, strikes, fires, labor or material shortages, mechanical difficulties, governmental restrictions, and acts of God, notice of termination shall be effective only after ABC shall have continued its failure to reprint for a three (3) month period after termination of the situation which prevented ABC's compliance with the Author's demand.

(b) The Work shall not be deemed "out of print" within the meaning of this paragraph as long as it is available for sale through normal retail and wholesale channels in either hardcover or paperback editions from ABC or its licensee.

A: Is there a problem in the Out of Print clause?

L: This is the clause usually used by publishers. The issue is whether the book should be considered "in print" if there are copies available in Persian by the Iranian publisher who has a license. The answer is obviously "no." This provision is made better balanced by defining that the book "is in print if it is available from ABC in hardcover or in paperback in the U.S.," or another definition that makes the book generally available in sufficient quantity to meet normal sales requirements in the main territory. The author and publisher should set minimum unit sales to be achieved by a publisher in any one year. If the publisher fails to achieve these minimum sales, the rights will automatically revert to the author.

14. Author's Property.

ABC shall be responsible for only the same care of any property of the Author in its hands as it takes of its own. The Author shall retain copies of the manuscript and any other documents or materials supplied to ABC. If the Author does not present ABC with a written request for their return, ABC, after publication of the Work, may dispose of the original manuscript and proofs.

A: This looks acceptable to me.

L: Yes, we're now getting into a series of paragraphs that are fairly standard and generally acceptable.

15. Author's Copies.

ABC agrees to give the Author twenty (20) free copies of the regular edition of the Work and five (5) free copies of any paperback edition published by ABC. The Author may purchase additional copies of the Work for the Author's personal use at a discount of forty percent (40%) of list price. The cost of the copies ordered by the Author will be charged to his/her royalty account unless there are not sufficient accrued royalties owed to the Author to pay for the ordered copies. In such case, the Author shall enclose payment with the order.

L: In passing, let me mention that some paperback houses will give the author thirty free copies of the book or a paperback original.

16. Licenses.

ABC agrees to promptly advise the Author of the terms of any grants or licenses made by it with respect to the Work whenever the Author's share of the proceeds or royalty is likely to exceed one thousand dollars ($1000.00).

17. <u>Permissions.</u>

ABC may permit others to reprint portions of the Work. Any payments received for such permissions shall be equally divided between the Author and ABC; however, ABC may grant permission without compensation to publish extracts from the Work containing 500 words or less in order to promote the sale of the Work. Such payment will be included as a separate item on the royalty statement.

18. <u>Author's Agent.</u>

The Author hereby authorizes his/her agent ("Agent") to collect and receive all sums of money payable to the Author under this Agreement. The payment to the Author's Agent shall fully and validly discharge ABC from its obligations to pay the Author such sums of money. The Agent may also act on the Author's behalf in all matters arising out of this Agreement, including, but not limited to, amendment of this Agreement and settlement of any controversies arising out of this Agreement. ABC may rely on the Agent in such matters until ABC has received written notice from the Author that terminates the agency. Upon the receipt of such notice, ABC shall pay all further sums payable pursuant to this Agreement directly to the Author or any other person(s) as the Author shall direct in writing.

A: How does this affect me since I do not have an agent?

L: Delete this paragraph. In case you do have an agent some time in the future, do not use this paragraph. All you need to do is have 10 or 15 percent—or whatever you agree upon as an agent's fee—paid directly to the agent and your money paid directly to you. You generally would not wish the agent to act on your behalf on all matters. You should be informed directly by the publisher of areas of concern arising out of the agreement and you will then consult your agent or lawyer as you see fit.

The following nine provisions are "lawyers' provisions" that should not concern you. They are necessary to make the contract complete and are useful if a dispute arises.

19. Entire Agreement.

This Agreement contains the entire agreement of the parties in regard to the subject matter hereof, supersedes all prior agreements and understandings of the parties, and may be changed only by a written document signed by the party against whom enforcement of any waiver, change, modification, extension, or discharge is sought.

20. Severability.

If any provision of this Agreement shall be prohibited by or invalid under applicable law, such provision shall be ineffective to the extent of such prohibition or invalidity without invalidating the remainder of such provision or the remaining provisions of this Agreement.

21. Further Documents.

The Author agrees to execute and deliver to ABC any and all documents in proper or customary form necessary or helpful to the use, sale, license, or other disposition of any or all the rights granted to ABC herein, or for more fully carrying out the purposes and intent of this Agreement. The Author hereby irrevocably appoints ABC as his/her attorney-in-fact to execute any such documents.

22. Notices.

Any notice required to be given, served, or delivered to any of the parties hereto shall be sufficient if it is in writing and sent certified or registered mail, with proper postage prepaid, addressed as follows:

To ABC:

ABC Publishing, Inc.
Pumpkin Ridge Road
Rye, New York 10580
Attn: Maureen Sheehan, President

To Author:

Mary K. Smith
605 Third Avenue
New York, New York 10158

or to other such address as a party from time to time may designate by notice to the other as herein before provided.

23. Remedies.

No course of dealing between or among the parties to this Agreement, any failure or delay on the part of any party in exercising any remedy of such party or any other party, or no single or partial exercise of any remedy hereunder shall operate as a waiver or preclude the exercise of any other remedy available to either of the parties.

24. Survival of Rights.

(a) In the event of the termination of this Agreement as elsewhere provided herein, any rights reverting to the Author shall be subject to all licenses and other grants of rights previously made by ABC to third parties as well as ABC's rights to the proceeds under those third party agreements subject, however, to payment to the Author for his/her share of such proceeds.

(b) In addition to the rights set forth above in subparagraph (a), the following paragraphs shall survive termination: Author's Property, Warranty and Indemnification, Author's Agent, Assignment, Further Documents, Remedies, Notices, Entire Agreement, Applicable Law, Headings, and Royalty Statements and Payments.

25. Assignment.

This Agreement shall be binding upon and inure to the benefit of the successors and assigns of ABC and the successors, heirs, and estate of the Author. Since this Agreement is for personal services, the Author may not assign or delegate any duties or obligations under this Agreement, however, he/she may assign any net sums due to him/her hereunder. ABC may assign this Agreement if it sells all or substantially all of its assets.

26. Applicable Law.

This Agreement shall be governed by and construed in accordance with the internal substantive laws of the State of New York and the parties hereby consent to the jurisdiction of the courts over the matters relating to this Agreement.

27. Headings.

The headings in this Agreement are for convenience of reference only and shall not limit or otherwise affect the meaning hereof.

Agreed this _____ day of _____ , 20___ , by:

_____
                                              Author

S.S.# _____

_____
                                              Publisher

L: Of all the "lawyer's provisions," the only one that I would try to change would be number 26, "Applicable Law." This provision means that any dispute that cannot be resolved by the parties must go to court, an expensive and time-consuming process. An easier course being followed by some publishers is to provide for arbitration, which can be done in an informal setting. The disputants agree on an arbitrator, they argue the merits of their case without a lawyer if they prefer, and the arbitrator makes a decision based upon fairness. If you could, I would suggest you try to get the following paragraph substituted for the paragraph shown above:

Arbitration.

Any controversy or claim arising out of or relating to this agreement, or the breach hereof, shall be settled by arbitration in New York City, in accordance with the rules of the American Arbitration Association. Judgment upon the award rendered may be entered in any court having jurisdiction thereof. The costs of the arbitration shall be borne equally by the parties thereto.

L: Finally, some advice about electronic rights. You may expect to see something much like this in the future:

Grant of Electronic Rights.

The Author grants to the Publisher the exclusive right to create, distribute, and license electronic rights as described below:

(i) the right to encompass or enhance any material or aspect of the Work in a format as illustrated by a "floppy" disc, CD-ROM, electronic book, or any other format now known or to be developed in the future.

(ii) the right to transmit the Work by broadcast, public display, transmission networks, or any other form of transmission now known or to be developed in the future.

(iii) the right to utilize any medium to reinterpret the Work in print, in an optical or graphical form, or in any other medium now known or to be developed in the future.

The Author agrees that should an electronic application of the Work not included in this grant become known, at the written request of the Publisher, the Author will grant the exclusive right to the Publisher and the compensation to the Author shall be determined by relating the new right to existing rights or, if this is not possible, by mutual agreement.

L: This is a provision currently appearing in some publishers' contracts. It has generated strong objection from The Authors Guild. The grant is sweeping and the payment terms difficult to administer. If the publisher has made a significant investment in a new technology effort, the author might agree to this provision and trust that there will be a reasonable exploitation of her rights and a fair payment. The author should attempt to control the utilization of these rights by seeking prior approval of the use of electronic rights.

The Authors Guild's position in this matter includes three conditions: (1) fair compensation on the traditional advance and royalty basis, that is, payment per use or sale; (2) when rights are licensed by the publisher to another party, the author should be compensated by the publisher on the traditional basis of an agent's commission, with the author receiving 85 to 90 percent; and (3) no use of a work should be made without the author's approval of medium, format, and content.

Electronic publishing is evolving rapidly and significantly, and the next decade should see more standardized terms in this area that are acceptable to both publisher and author. I advise the first-time author to ask for something similar to The Authors Guild's recommendation—and to be happy with what she can get.

A: What is your final word of advice?

L: Relax. The main issue is to get your book published with enthusiasm by the publisher. One good technique to eliminate many of the points of negotiation is to ask the publisher to make the changes he would normally make if the issue were raised by his best author. I have found that, in order to save the negotiating time, the publisher will often make some changes that will improve the contract to your benefit. The publisher wishes to maintain a cordial relationship with you because he hopes that there are many more books to come. Do not expect to get major concessions, but whatever you get, put these issues out of the negotiations. You can then concentrate on those issues that trouble you and ones not resolved.

Remember, this is only one book, and if you are successful you can always improve the contract in the negotiations for your next book.

A: This certainly has been an education for me. While I feel better prepared, I still think I need a lawyer.

L: I think you're right. However, with your increased contract literacy (from Chapter 9) and this review of a sample contract, you should be able to save the lawyer's time and reduce the lawyer's fee.

A: How many changes do you think I will be able to make in this contract?

L: As a first-time author, not many. The publisher realizes that he must continue to seek out and publish new authors. He also realizes that publishing new authors is a substantial risk. Publishers often lose money on first-time authors and, as a result, publishers wish to obtain the broadest grant of rights and the most favorable economic terms to minimize their risk. And if they have made a bad initial judgment in selecting the book and the manuscript, when received, is not satisfactory, they want to be relieved of their responsibility to publish the book at the least cost.

In general, most publishers are fair-minded and understand the role of the author in their future. If you can address the issues in a principled manner, explaining the merits of your position, you will find the publisher will meet you more than halfway. Go into the negotiations with a working knowledge of publishing law and a positive, open manner and you will get a fair contract.

11

Reprise

From the first chapter, the goal of this book has been to help you get your manuscript published. In this game, a silver medal does not count. Praise from an editor is not as meaningful as praise from a reader of your published book. Winners are those writers who are published.

This book has focused on submitting a quality manuscript and the Eight-Step Program for Selling Your Book:

1. Write a Winning Proposal.

2. Find the Best Publisher.

3. Submit Your Book to the Right Editor.

4. Use the Two P's—Patience and Persistence.

5. Use the Rejection Profitably.

6. Keep Moving. Network. Make Contacts.

7. Think Small.

8. Keep Reading.

At this point, as our time together has almost come to an end, I add one more step:

9. Keep Writing.

If you continue to get rejections after having reworked your manuscript with help and researched carefully to find the right publisher and right editor, do not be discouraged. Keep your day job, but keep writing.

For solace, read *Rotten Rejections*, edited by André Bernard. If you are not succeeding at first, you are part of a fraternity of writers whose works were initially rejected. The list of those writers include: Stephen King, who was told the genre in which he was writing "would not sell"; John Le Carré, who was told he had "no future"; Norman Mailer, admonished that his writing would "set back publishing twenty-five years"; and Ayn Rand, who was advised that her work was "unsalable and unpublishable."

Rejection of manuscripts is a part of the publishing process. The tastes and sensitivities of editors vary. Public tastes change. Editors often have a difficult time explaining why they select a particular manuscript. They often say, "It just feels right."

If you feel strongly about your book, you can even do what Pat Conroy, the author of *The Prince of Tides*, did when no one would publish his first book, and self-publish.

Self-publishing has become easier (and more respectable) by using services that will edit, print, publish, and distribute on the author's behalf. The list of successful books that have been initially self-published include *The Christmas Box*, *A Time to Kill*, and *The Celestine Prophecy*. There are also services that will enable an author to publish directly on the Web.

Whatever you do, maintain a positive attitude and take the ninth step in the program to sell your book—keep writing.

The Tool Kit:
Appendixes A–D

These four appendixes provide the tools you will need to be expert as an author-agent. They are:

A. PubSpeak—The Publishing Industry's Private Language: A Glossary

B. How to Use *Literary Market Place* to Find Your Publisher, Editor, and Leading Publishers by Category

C. Best Bets—The Publishers Most Likely to Read and Accept Your Book

D. Manuscript Submission Record

APPENDIX A

PubSpeak—
The Publishing Industry's Private
Language: A Glossary

Publishers have their own special language, which I call PubSpeak. Many words and phrases have special meaning in publishing. There are also abbreviations that stand for associations important to the life of authors and editors. Most first-time authors, to hide their newness to the publishing fraternity, hide their lack of knowledge of these special terms. Now you can be an insider too.

AA—Author's Alterations. Changes that the author makes after the galley proofs are provided by the publisher. Most publisher-author contracts stipulate a penalty if the author's changes are excessive.

AAP—Association of American Publishers. The industry association of book publishers, primarily the larger publishers. Smaller publishers are organized into regional associations or by specialty.

AAUP—Association of American University Presses. The publishers associated with colleges and universities who publish both scholarly and popular trade books.

ABA—American Booksellers Association. The trade association for the booksellers in the United States, providing a number of important services and training for bookseller members.

Advance—Moneys paid to the author prior to publication to be earned from royalties on sales. This same term is used by publishers to indicate the number of copies ordered prior to publication of a book (e.g., "We expected to advance 20,000 copies of the total printing of 40,000 copies.").

Agent—Hardly needs definition, but just in case, an independent representative of an author or other creative artist who sells the author's or artist's work to a third party and receives a commission on the sale, usually 10 to 15 percent. Some agents, especially those building a clientele, will represent unpublished authors. The term of the agency may extend over a number of works or on a single-book basis. The author-agent agreement should be in writing.

ALA—American Library Association. An organization of librarians providing services to librarians. The ALA holds two excellent trade shows a year where publishers and others who sell to libraries meet.

Auction—This is a process used by publishers (and authors on occasion) to ask other publishers to bid for rights, such as the paperback or book club rights. Bids are usually made by telephone in sequence, advancing by predetermined dollar amounts until only one publisher, the winner, remains. There is a high degree of trust between publishers, allowing this process to be the primary method of selling valuable rights.

Backlist—Titles that have been published previous to the current season and continue to sell sufficient copies to keep the book in print.

BEA—The annual trade show attended by most publishers. BEA is the abbreviation for Book Expo America.

Book Club—Marketing organization that sells books to its members. The conventional view that Book-of-the-Month Club and the other widely advertised clubs are the primary customers for these rights is no longer valid. The Book-of-the-Month Club itself has diversified. There are many important specialized book clubs; for example, Scholastic Publishing has a major business in book clubs selling children's books to classrooms. Book clubs acquire the rights from the holder of the rights (usually the publisher), and pay an advance and royalty. The rights are often auctioned. Bertelsmann now owns most of the major book club organizations in the United States and is strong abroad. The clubs Bertelsmann owns have been combined under a new entity called Bookspan.

CD-ROM—Compact disc–read only memory. A compact disc on which a program has been recorded that usually stores a vast amount of text combined with other media, such as video clips, photographic images, and sound. The disc is similar in size and shape to an audio compact disc (CD), but can only be played in a compact disc player that is installed in a computer (called a CD-ROM drive). "Read only memory" means that you can't alter or add to the disc's contents.

College Store—A bookstore located on or near a college campus, serving the students and faculty (and sometimes the public). Some stores are owned by the university; others are operated under a lease from the university by private corporations that specialize in operating college bookstores.

Cooperative Advertising—Ads run by a bookseller in which part of the cost is paid by a publisher. This is an important means of getting stock into a bookstore and announcing the availability of the book to the public.

Copyediting—Careful review of a manuscript prior to publication by an expert in grammar, punctuation, sentence structure, and clarity. This is a function performed by the publisher at his expense. The results of copyediting are furnished to the author for review and acceptance.

Copyright—This is a property right possessed by the author once the work is fixed in any tangible form (e.g., typed, handwritten, filmed, etc.). Copyright does not protect "ideas," only the author's particular expression of those ideas. Under the present law, copyright is not lost if notice ("c" in a circle[©]) is omitted. Registration with the Copyright Office is only required if you sue for infringement. However, authors are well advised to take those steps to identify their ownership. The author owns a "bundle of rights" under copyright. These rights may be conveyed separately. If the rights granted are exclusive, the grant must be in writing. The term of the copyright is the life of the author plus seventy years. However, even if the grant to the publisher is for the full term of the copyright, the author has a right to terminate any license after thirty-five years. For further information write the Register of Copyrights, United States Copyright Office, Library of Congress, Washington, DC 20559.

El-Hi—The educational market covering elementary grades (kindergarten to grade eight) and high school (grades nine through twelve).

Fair Use—The right, under Section 107 of the Copyright Act, to use materials, published or unpublished, in a carefully restricted manner without permission of the copyright holder. Use of another's copyrighted material in the author's work, without permission, is not a decision an author should take without legal advice. The concept of "fair use" is too complicated to explain in a sentence. In deciding whether you wish to use another's work, the question you should ask yourself is "If I were the author of the work and another author used my work, would I think it is fair? Would the use of the material being used have a negative effect on the sale of my work?" To be safe, ask for permission before copying from another work.

Foreign Rights—The rights owned by the author, which can be conveyed to the publisher in writing, to publish her book outside the United States, either on her own or through a license with a foreign publisher.

Frankfurt Book Fair—The largest international book fair in the world, attracting publishers from many countries; held in Frankfurt am Main, Germany, usually in October each year.

Galleys—Refers to the first proofs of typeset materials and are the first time a manuscript appears set in type. Formerly, the galleys were long sheets on which two or three pages would appear; now most galleys appear on $8^1/2 \times$ 11-inch paper. In other instances, galleys are bound, usually uncorrected, and appear in actual page size. Unbound galleys are used for copyediting; bound galleys are used for advance reading by those who need to read the book far ahead of publication (reviewers, important buyers) in order to support its publication.

Guarantee—Normally used as an advance guarantee, which means that the advance on royalties belongs to the author as long as the publisher accepts the book for publication. Sometimes it is referred to in a contract as "nonrecoverable advance." This means that no matter how few copies are sold, the author will, at a minimum, receive the guaranteed amount of money for her work.

Imprint—The name of a publisher (or its division or subsidiary) used to identify the books he publishes; normally shown on the spine of the book, the jacket, and title page.

Jacket—Designed paper cover over a bound book, sometimes referred to as a dust jacket. The author is often consulted by the publisher on the jacket design since it is a primary selling tool for the book at point of sale.

Juvenile—A shorthand way of referring to a book written for children (e.g., juvenile books).

List—The books published by a publisher that are currently in print. When used as the publisher's list, it refers to the catalog of the publisher.

Literary Agent—See *Agent*.

LMP—*Literary Market Place.* The annual directory of publishers and the entire industry, published by R. R. Bowker. If you are unfamiliar with this book, go to your public library reference section and study it. It is an invaluable tool for someone who wishes to be her own agent. See Appendix B for more information as to content and use.

Logo—Trademark or indicia used by the publisher to identify his company.

Mail Order—Usually associated with direct-mail sales. Certain books can be sold directly to the buyer through advertisements offering the book, or through direct-mail letters addressed to potential buyers. Books are then shipped through the mail.

Mass Market—There are an estimated 100,000 retail stores in which books are sold that are not traditional bookstores (some examples are supermarkets, drugstores, and warehouse outlets) and this market is defined as the mass market. Previously, mass market outlets sold only paperbacks and lower-priced children's books. Not so today. However, rack-sized paperbacks are often referred to as mass market paperbacks to distinguish them from the trade paperbacks generally sold only in bookstores.

Multimedia—Refers to products in which print, illustration, sound, and film are mixed, generally for utilization in a computer. See also *CD-ROM*.

OP (Out of Print)—Refers to those books that are out of print and no longer available in the publisher's stock.

Option—A commitment that the current publisher can acquire a subsequent work of an author prior to that work being made available to competing publishers. Term may also apply to licenses. For instance, a primary publisher commits to a secondary publisher (who has licensed certain rights to an author's work) that he will be given first opportunity to obtain the same rights to a subsequent work before it is offered to competing publishers.

Paperback—A book bound with a paper cover (usually illustrated), as opposed to a book which has a hard, board binding. See also *Mass Market*.

Permission—The right to use previously published or as yet unpublished material in a work with suitable acknowledgment to the author granting the permission. The permission to use the material is usually obtained from the Permissions Department of the originating publisher. A fee may be required. To facilitate clearances of material primarily in journals, there is a Copyright Clearance Center from which permissions can be sought.

Professional Books—Created primarily for professionals, such as doctors, nurses, and engineers.

Publicity—An activity other than space and cooperative advertising, undertaken by a publisher to make the public aware of an author's book. This include such measures as author tours, book signings, posters, review copy mailings, catalogs, etc.

PW—*Publishers Weekly*, the primary weekly industry trade publication. This is essential for authors and especially those authors who wish to be their own agent. Available in most public libraries and on line at www.publishersweekly.com.

Religious Books—Traditionally referred to Bibles, prayer books, hymnals, testaments, and other sacred books. Recently the definition has been expanded to include inspirational books with religious underpinnings and other books that guide readers in the exploration and practice of many of the world's religions and philosophies.

Remainders—Books that the publisher cannot sell at the full price through normal channels that are offered, as long as the stock remains, to the retailers at a sharply lower price, and which the retailer offers to the public at a fraction of the regular selling price. In some instances, these so-called remainder books are created to provide the consumer a good value. In other instances, a book unsuccessful at the full price finds a new and continuing market at the lower price and stays in print for a longer period of time as a remainder.

Reprint—A new printing of the book by the original publisher or a printing of the book by a licensed publisher. In the first instance, the publisher watches the sales data, and before the supply of the book is exhausted, orders a reprint using the original production materials stored at the printer. In the second instance, the original publisher feels that he has exhausted all efforts to sell to his market and finds another publisher who specializes in reprinting previously published books. Printing technology now makes it possible to print as few as fifty copies economically and to price them so a reader may acquire them. This is useful for an author to know so she can encourage a publisher to keep her book available to the public.

Reserve—An accounting procedure used by publishers to provide for a future expense contemplated by the publisher. A return reserve is an estimate of the expense to be incurred when books are returned.

Returns—Books that are unsold and returned by the retailer or wholesaler to the publisher. Some booksellers buy books on a nonreturnable basis and are given a price incentive, but essentially all books are returnable at the option of the bookseller, within some general standards set by the publisher. Alfred Knopf, one of the great men in publishing, disparagingly said the policy was typified by the statement, "Gone today and here tomorrow." The author should not be concerned because the publisher withholds royalty payments (a "return reserve") to offset potential returns. Ultimately, after all the returns are in, the author receives the money due her in a final accounting.

Review Copy—Free copies sent to established book reviewers for newspapers and magazines. The publisher has a list of reviewers and is hopeful that the receipt of a copy will generate interest. Reviews in newspapers and periodicals are an essential part of the promotion of a book.

Royalties—The amount received by an author based upon sales of her book. Royalties are expressed in a percentage of the retail price (the suggested price printed on the jacket of the book). Sometimes, royalties are based upon the net receipts (the price of the book as shown in a publisher's catalog less the bookstore's discount, generally 40 to 45 percent) or, in the case of nonbookstore sales, a percentage of the publisher's receipts (e.g., special sales where they may be 10 percent of the net received). Royalties that are earned by sales are offset against the advance payment. Earned royalties must surpass the advance before the author receives additional royalty payments.

Scholarly Books—A broad designation to cover books in highly specialized areas of knowledge that are designed essentially for a limited market, although some books of note occasionally move over to the trade list.

Serialization—Magazines and newspapers often condense a book or select important sections of a book and publish them. If the magazine or newspaper is allowed to do this prior to publication of the book, it is first serialization; if serialization appears after the book has been released, it is second serialization. This is an important distinction, because in the former case the author receives 85 to 90 percent of the income; in the latter case, the income is usually shared equally with the publisher.

Slush Pile—See *Unsolicited Manuscript.*

Space Advertising—Paid ads placed by the publisher in newspapers and magazines promoting the book.

Special Sales—Sales of the book made by the publisher to accounts outside of bookstores, often in large quantities at low prices and with a lower royalty to the author.

Subscription Reference Books—Multivolume encyclopedias or specialized reference books marketed by door-to-door salesmen or by direct-mail offers. Customers agree to buy the entire set.

Subsidiary Rights—Rights derived from the literary work and owned by the author (other than the primary right to publish the literary work). For example, if the author conveys only hardcover publication rights in the English language to the United States and Canada, all other rights such as translation, foreign sales, paperback, book club publication, etc., are subsidiary rights.

Textbooks—Books created by publishers specializing in the educational market for adoption for use in elementary and high schools. Sales are made directly to school districts. Books created for colleges and universities are sold to students through college bookstores.

Title Page—The page at the beginning of the book, normally on the right side, which sets forth the title, the author, and publisher. The reverse side of the title page, the copyright page, normally contains the copyright notice and other essential information to assist the reader in reaching the publisher if necessary.

Trade Books—Books created primarily for the general reader to be sold to the public through bookstores.

Trade Discount—The percentage that the publisher will reduce the price to provide a margin for the trade seller of the book. The schedules of trade discounts vary by publishers and are further complicated by incentives to buy on a nonreturnable basis.

Trade Paperback—Normally a softcover reprint of a hardcover trade book in approximately the same size as the trade book (often printed from the same plates) that is sold at a lower price in a retail bookstore because it has a soft cover.

University Press—A publishing firm sponsored by a university. In all respects, this entity is like other publishers, except for the character of the books published, which is generally scholarly.

Unsolicited Manuscript—Manuscript submitted to the publisher directly by the author (not through an agent) without invitation from the publisher. In trade parlance these unsolicited manuscripts are sometimes referred to as the "Slush Pile" or as manuscripts received "over the transom." The essential distinction is that the manuscript is not commissioned or sought by the editor.

Vanity Publishing—Publication done by a publisher who requires that the author pay for all the costs of publication and distribution as well as "overhead costs." If the prospects for publication by a conventional publisher are remote, the author is better advised to self-publish rather than use a vanity publisher. There are a number of excellent books on self-publishing, and assistance is available from organizations that are involved in self-publishing.

APPENDIX B

How to Use *Literary Market Place* to Find Your Publisher, Editor, and Leading Publishers by Category

Your single most important reference source to locate the publishers to whom you should send your proposal and the name of the editor to whom the proposal should be addressed is *Literary Market Place*, referred to by those in the know as *LMP.* It also can serve many other useful purposes.

The thick volume has more than two thousand pages and is published annually by R. R. Bowker. *LMP* is available at most public libraries. Since book publishing seems to be in constant motion with mergers and acquisitions, and editors often move from one house to another, other trade sources such as *Publishers Weekly* should be used to update information in *LMP* between annual editions. You can update the information in *LMP* through *Publishers Weekly* (also published by R. R. Bowker) or by making a telephone call to the publisher and editor you have chosen. If she has moved to a new job, the editorial assistant will often give you the name of the person to whom you should send your proposal. (The entries from *LMP* that follow are for illustration only and may be out of date. Do not use this information to locate a publisher or editor.)

You will find these examples of sections of *LMP* useful to you.

The List of U.S. Book Publishers

This is an alphabetical list of all the small, midsized, and large publishers in the United States. This is essential information. Below is a sample of what you will find, and how to use it. Directory information provides you with the address and telephone number of whom to send your adult hardcover manuscript.

Henry Holt & Co Inc
Unit of Holtzbrinck Publishing Holdings
115 W 18 St., New York NY 10011
SAN: 200-2108

Tel: 212-886-9200; Fax: 212-633-0748
E-mail: publicity@hholt.com
Web site: www.henryholt.com

Pres. & Publisher: John Sterling
V.P., Fin. and Admin: George Rubich
V.P., Sales & Mktg: Maggie Richards
V.P., Creative Director: Raquel Jarmillo
Dir. of Publicity: Elisabeth Shreve
Dir. of Advertising and Promotion: Lucille Rettino
Dir. of National Accounts: B. J. Gabriel
Dir. of Special Markets: Judith Sisko
Intl. & Subsidiary Rights: Denise Cronin
Dir. of Permissions: Mimi Ross
Dir. of Operations: Deborah Valcourt
Managerial Director: Nancy Clements
Executive Ed: David Sobel
Ed., Adult Trade: Elizabeth Stein
Associate Publisher, John Macrae Books: John Macrae
Associate Publisher, Metropolitan Books: Sarah Bershtel

Editor, Metropolitan Books: Riva Hochermann
Associate Publisher, Books for Young Readers: Laura Goodwin
Executive Editor, Books for Young Readers: Nina Ignatowicz
Sr. Ed., Books for Young Readers: Marc Aronson; Christy
    Ottaviano
Executive Dir. Mktg., Books for Young Readers: Beth Feldman

Founded 1866
Total Titles: 3000 in print

Henry Holt & Company, LLC., one of America's foremost publishers, was founded in 1866. Based in New York City, Holt publishes approximately 175 books a year, including hardcover fiction and nonfiction; Owl Books (its trade paperback division); Books for Young Readers; Metropolitan Books; and Times Books.

Throughout its history, Holt has published such important writers as Robert Frost, A. E. Housman, Norman Mailer, Kurt Vonnegut, Philip Roth, James Baldwin, and Sue Grafton, to name a few. Holt's current authors include Pulitzer Prize winners David Levering Lewis and Robert Olen Butler, national best-selling author Thomas Pynchon, and many others.

How to Use LMP

To use *LMP*, the management information is of no use to you at present. Your interest is in finding a name to whom you can send your manuscript. If you have a novel or a nonfiction book, your best bet would be to address this to **Editor of Adult Trade: Elizabeth Stein.** The Executive Editor is at too high a level and the other editorial staff work in discrete and specialized areas. If your manuscript belongs in any of the other imprints, it is likely that the Adult Trade editor would forward this to the appropriate person.

If you have a juvenile manuscript, the best choice would be **Senior Editor: Books for Young Readers: Marc Aronson or Christy Ottaviano.** These individuals would have the time to devote and would probably read your manuscript. The others listed would likely be too busy to give it the attention you wish

This personnel information provides you with a choice. Since the editor-in-chief would rarely be a first reader, any of the other editors might be chosen but your best bet is the senior editor.

Finding Your Way Around the Conglomerates

Over the last two decades three large publishers, Random House, Penguin Putnam, and Simon & Schuster have acquired smaller publishers so that together they comprise 44 percent of all trade sales. Fortunately, *LMP* lists the various subsidiaries or divisions of these major houses separately. For example, at the end of the Random House entry you will find a list of the twenty-six companies owned by Random House. At the end of the Penguin Putnam entry there is a list of twenty-eight companies.

Fortunately, the subsidiaries of Random House as well as the subsidiaries of the other mega-publishers allow publishing decisions to be made at the operating level. There is a separate entry for each of the publishing units owned by Random House, Penguin Putnam, as well as the other conglomerates so you can find the appropriate publisher and within the publisher the right editor for your book.

As a further help in finding the right publishing unit within the conglomerate it is useful to note that each of the smaller publishers acquired by conglomerate publishers have their own specialty. (Most of these units have their own Web page that describes the category in which they publish.) This helps in matching the publisher to your manuscript. Once you find the right publisher you can easily find an editor to whom you can send your manuscript.

For example, Fodor's Travel Publications is a part of the Random House family and is listed in *LMP* at the end of the Random

House entry. If you have a travel-related book, you should go to the entry in *LMP* for Fodor's. You will find that this entry looks remarkably the same as the listing for Holt. Once again, you will find the names of all the editorial staff, and with some study you can then find the appropriate person to whom to send your book.

This same top-down technique should be used in identifying sources within all the conglomerates. The editors within these specialized publishing units are easy to reach and responsive. You can find good potential buyers for your manuscript by following the trail, within the pages of *LMP* from the parent company, the top, down to each of the subsidiaries.

Leading Publishers by Category

To help you target your efforts to find the right publisher for your book, I have listed the leading publishers in a variety of fields. They are listed in alphabetical order. You can find the address of the publisher in *LMP* and the name of the editor to whom you should send your manuscript in the listing. Publishers understand that you will be submitting your manuscript to more than one publisher simultaneously. They would, as a matter of courtesy, appreciate knowing if you are making a simultaneous submission.

Leading Travel Book Publishers

Abbeville Press
Ballantine
Berlitz
Countryman Press
Fodor's (Random House)
Foghorn Press
Frommer's (Macmillan)
Globe Pequot Press
Landmark Guidebooks
Langenscheidt Publishing
Lonely Planet
Moon Publications
NTC/Contemporary
Penguin Putnam
Rough Guides
Simon & Schuster
Trafalgar Square

Leading Business Book Publishers

Addison-Wesley	Little, Brown
Amacom	McGraw-Hill
HarperCollins	Penguin Putnam
Houghton Mifflin	Random House
Hyperion	Simon & Schuster
John Wiley & Sons	

Leading Personal Finance/Investing Book Publishers

Addison-Wesley	Little, Brown
Amacom	McGraw-Hill
HarperCollins	Penguin Putnam
Houghton Mifflin	Random House
Hyperion	Simon & Schuster
John Wiley & Sons	

Leading Computer Book Publishers

Abacus	McGraw-Hill
Addison-Wesley	Microsoft Press
HarperCollins	Penguin Putnam
Henry Holt	Random House
Houghton Mifflin	Simon & Schuster
Hungry Minds	Thomson Corporation
John Wiley & Sons	Wolff New Media

Leading Religious Book Publishers

Abingdon
Bantam Doubleday Dell
Bethany House
Chrysalis Books
DK
HarperSanFrancisco
Herald Press
Hyperion
Perigee

Putnam Berkley
Random House
Riverhead Press
Rodale Press
Simon & Schuster
Thomas Nelson
Tyndale House
Warner Books
Zondervan

Leading Romance Book Publishers

Avon
Bantam
Harlequin
HarperCollins
Kensington

Penguin Putnam
Pocket Books
Random House
Warner Books

Leading Mystery Book Publishers

Avon
Ballantine
Bantam Doubleday Dell
Berkley Prime Crime
Breese Books
Crown
Delacorte
Dutton
Fawcett
HarperCollins
Kensington

Little, Brown
Morrow
Mysterious Press (Warner)
Penguin Putnam
Picardy Press
Scribner
Simon & Schuster
St. Martin's/Dead Letter
Walker
Write Way Publishing

Leading Trade Reference Book Publishers

Bantam Doubleday Dell   Macmillan
Chelsea House   McGraw-Hill
DK   Merriam Webster
Facts on File   Penguin Putnam
HarperCollins   Random House
Henry Holt   Simon & Schuster
Houghton Mifflin

Leading Cookbook Publishers

Avery   Meredith
Berkley Publishing   Penguin Putnam
Chronicle   Random House
DK   Reader's Digest
GT Publishing   Simon & Schuster
HarperCollins   Time Inc.
Little, Brown   William Morrow
Macmillan

Indexes

LMP has three indexes that are helpful. Publishers are organized:

1. Geographically by state

2. By type of publication (typical listings are: Association Presses, Audio Cassettes, A.V. Materials, Bibliographies, Braille Books, Databases, and Dictionaries & Encyclopedias)

3. By subject (typical entries are: Accounting, Advertising, Aeronautics, and Aviation)

Under each heading, there is a one-line listing or the publisher's name. To find more detailed information concerning the publisher, you must go back to the alphabetical listing in the front of the book.

The difficulty with these listings is that there are too many publishers listed in each category. A significant amount of work is required to find the most desirable publishers in each category to whom to submit your work.

Small Presses

There is a limited listing of small presses which might be helpful when your book is designed for a limited, specific market. There is a more complete listing available from the Small Press Center at 20 West 44th Street, New York, NY 10036; Tel: 212-764-7021; Fax: 212-354-5365.

Literary Agents

This is an excellent listing, albeit somewhat discouraging. In almost every instance, the agents' listings say, "No unsolicited mss, query first." There are additional directories of agents available, but this one is extensive and useful.

Calendar of Book Trade and Professional Events

This is a listing by month of events, many of which are useful for the first-time author. Major events such as the trade exhibits of the American Booksellers Association and the American Library Association are listed with the current venues and specific dates. The

Regional Book Exhibits are listed, as well as meetings for specialists such as the Garden Writers Association of America. This is an extremely valuable listing.

Writers Conferences and Workshops

Many of the writers conferences, with information as to the sponsorship, the dates held, and the location appear in this listing. The Guide to Writers Conferences can be ordered from Shaw Guides, 625 Biltmore Way, Suite 1406, Coral Gables, FL 33134. This is a better directory with more conferences shown and more complete information.

Yellow Pages

You can use the yellow pages to find the name, address, telephone number, and fax number of the editors. This is a useful index once you know the name of the individual. It does not, however, meet your primary need of identifying the editor to whom you should send your book. The main directory of publishers does this.

Since finding the *right publisher* and the *right editor* are crucial to the ultimate success of your endeavor, becoming familiar with *LMP* is essential. Spend an hour or more just getting to know the directory; it is extensive and is designed for use by publishers and booksellers, but the sections discussed above can be extremely useful to you as well.

While *LMP*, *Publishers Weekly*, and other printed information is valuable, even more important is your own Rolodex, or whatever device you use to store names, addresses, and telephone and fax numbers. Using *LMP* as a base, start your own Rolodex and add to the identifying information all the seemingly unimportant, but actually very important, information, such as the name of the editorial assistant or secretary and her telephone number when you discover it, and any information that will make the editorial needs more focused, for example, "prefers mysteries with unusual detectives." The most important tool of any agent is his Rolodex. It will be your most valuable tool as well.

APPENDIX C

Best Bets—
The Publishers Most Likely to Read and
Accept Your Book

The purpose of Best Bets is to call your attention to the smaller publishers whom you might otherwise have overlooked. These publishers have identified their interests and set the conditions under which they will read and accept manuscripts.

The selection of publishers is based chiefly on personal experience. There may be many other publishers who deserve to be here. While my notes will be helpful, you should send for a catalog, check their Web site, or arrange to see their display at the annual BEA Trade Exhibit. These are trade publishers, most of whom publish in hardcover and trade paperback. Check the address in the current *LMP* before you submit material.

The abbreviations used to indicate the types of books they publish are:

F	fiction	C	computer instruction
NF	nonfiction	CREF	consumer reference
J	juvenile	H	humor

Academy Chicago Publisher

363 W. Erie St.
Chicago, IL 60610
Telephone: 312-751-7300
Fax: 312-751-7306
E-mail: Academy363@aol.com
Web site: www.academychicago.com
Contact: President and Senior Editor Anita Miller

F, NF

This publisher has a special interest in books for women, as well as non-fiction, history, fiction, and neglected classics. Web site stresses importance of matching author with the correct publisher and states it does not publish books with explicit sex or violence, science fiction, or thrillers, nor does it publish cookbooks, horror, photography, or children's books—other than classics. Does not accept electronic submissions. Query letter, synopsis with first three or four consecutive chapters, and SASE. Agents not required and this publisher will deal with authors and direct submissions on an individual basis. Founded in 1975.

Adams Media Corp

260 Center St.
Holbrook, MA 02343
Telephone: 781-767-8100
Fax: 781-767-0994
Web site: www.adamsmedia.com
Contact: Editor-in-Chief Edward Walters

NF

General nonfiction, business, self-help, careers, psychology, women's issues, cooking, gift books, regional, personal finance, parenting, reference, relationships, weddings. With approximately 100 new titles per year, Adams Media products are widely available through bookstores and retailers. Adams Media Corporation accepts submissions directly from authors (including first-time authors) and also from literary agents. Do not send complete manuscripts, but query with a description of the intended market for the book; an explanation of why someone would want to buy the book; a summary of the author's background; a table of contents, as detailed as possible; and a sample chapter. Does not accept electronic submissions at this time. Founded in 1980.

Algonquin Books of Chapel Hill
Division of Workman Publishing Co., Inc.
Box 2225
Chapel Hill, NC 27515
Telephone: 919-967-0108
Fax: 919-933-0272
E-mail: suzie@algonquin.com
Web site: www.algonquin.com
Contact: Editorial Director Shannon Ravenel

F, NF

High-quality trade books, fiction and nonfiction. See their Web site before submitting. Founded in 1982 as a small independent trade publisher, Algonquin publishes attractively produced books with individual promotion and extensive marketing. Founding mission included statement that "quality that will be our foremost consideration, for we believe that it is still possible to publish worthy fiction and nonfiction that will also be financially profitable for author, publisher, and bookseller."

Allworth Press
10 E. 23 St., Suite 510
New York, NY 10010
Telephone: 212-777-8395
Fax: 212-777-8261
E-mail: pub@allworth.com
Web site: www.allworth.com
Contact: Publisher Tad Crawford

NF

Business and self-help books for artists, designers, photographers, authors, and film and performing artists, as well as books about business, money, and law for the general public. Also publishes the best of the classics and contemporary writing in art and graphic design. Query with a one- or two-page outline of a proposed book, even if the book has already been written. The outline should give a chapter-by-chapter summary of the book's contents. Query should indicate the author's background, the intended audience for the book, any books that might be considered competitive, and why this book will compete successfully with those books. If the book has been written, please include two sample chapters with the outline. Founded in 1989 by author, attorney, and artists' rights advocate Tad Crawford, Allworth Press today publishes twenty-six to thirty titles annually.

Avery

Imprint of Penguin Putnam Inc.

375 Hudson St.

New York, NY 10014

Telephone: 212-366-2000

Fax: 212-366-2666

E-mail: online@penguinputnam.com

Web site: www.penguinputnam.com

Contact: Executive Editor Laura Shepherd

NF

Penguin Putnam Inc. acquired Avery in 1999. Avery publishes books on health and nutrition, with complementary natural or alternative focus. Avery's extensive backlist includes the "industry bible" *Prescription for Nutritional Healing*. Avery was established in 1976 as a college textbook publisher specializing in niche areas. Its first general-interest book, *From Pregnancy to Parenthood*, became one of the top-selling books in the field. Through a series of alliances, most notably with Hippocrates Health Institute, Avery began a program of health books by notable authors. In 1990, Avery published *Juicing for Life*, which sold more than 800,000 copies in its first year and continues to be one of Avery's best-selling titles. At the same time, Avery acquired the rights to *Prescription for Nutritional Healing*, which has sold more than five million copies. These two books are the cornerstones of a publishing program dedicated primarily to complementary medicine, nutrition, and healthful cooking.

Thomas Bouregy & Co., Inc.
160 Madison Avenue
New York, NY 10016
Telephone: 212-598-0222; 800-223-5251
Fax: 212-979-1862
E-mail: avalonbooks@worldnet.att.net
Web site: www.avalonbooks.com
Contact: Editor Erin Cartwright

F

A good place for the first-time novelist to start, Thomas Bouregy & Co., Inc. specializes in romances, career romances, historical romances, mysteries, and westerns. Under its Avalon Books imprint, Thomas Bouregy & Company, Inc. publishes books that are wholesome adult fiction, suitable for family reading. Detailed writer's guidelines are available at its Web site and specify that its books do not contain graphic or premarital sex, profanity, or gory violence. Sexual violence of any kind is not acceptable. The protagonists should not be drinkers, although it is okay if the villains drink. Avoid using plots that involve drugs, drug smuggling, or drug lords. Thomas Bouregy & Co. publishes sixty books a year in bimonthly cycles of ten. A cycle consists of two career romances, two general romances, two historical romances, two mysteries, and two westerns. All the romances are contemporary; all the westerns are historical. The important action in all the books takes place over a relatively short period of time, ranging from days to no longer than a year. Books range from a minimum of 40,000 words to a maximum of 60,000 words (usually about 160 to 210 manuscript pages). Founded in 1950, Thomas Bouregy & Company accepts unagented material and multiple submissions; however, you should indicate that the proposal is a multiple submission. When submitting, include a query letter, a two- to three-page (and no longer) synopsis of the entire manuscript, and the first three chapters. All submissions must be typed and double-spaced. Include a SASE.

Carolrhoda Books, Inc.

Division of the Lerner Publishing Group
241 First Avenue N.
Minneapolis, MN 55401
Telephone: 612-332-3344, 800-328-4929
Fax: 612-332-7615
E-mail: info@lernerbooks.com
Web site: www.lernerbooks.com
Contact: Jennifer Zimian for Lerner Publications Company and Rebecca
    Poole for Carolrhoda Books

J

Carolrhoda Books features critically acclaimed and award-winning picture books, nonfiction, and fiction titles for children in grades K–6, including beginning readers, social studies, art, multicultural issues, biography, and activity books. Submissions to Carolrhoda Books, Inc. are accepted in the months of March and October only. Submissions received in any month other than March or October will be returned unopened to the sender. A SASE is required for all submissions and those submissions without SASEs will not receive any response. Allow two to six months for a response. No phone calls please. Carolrhoda no longer answers queries regarding the status of submissions. Carolrhoda does not publish alphabet books, puzzle books, song books, textbooks, workbooks, religious subject matter, or plays. Founded in 1969.

Chelsea House Publishers

1974 Sproul Road, Suite 400
Broomall, PA 19008-0914
Mailing address: P.O. Box 914
Broomall, PA 19008-0914
Telephone: 610-353-5166, 800-848-BOOK
Fax: 610-359-1439
E-mail: info@chelseahouse.com
Web site: www.chelseahouse.com
Contact: John Bevilacqua

J

Chelsea publishes children and young adult titles for the library and the curriculum market. It is a good buyer for serious juvenile books, especially in the multicultural area. For over thirty years, Chelsea House has published high-quality nonfiction with an abundance of biographies, histories, multicultural studies, and many other types of books for children and young adults, as well as hundreds of volumes of literary criticism and references for older readers. Founded in 1966.

Chronicle Books
85 Second St., Sixth Floor
San Francisco, CA 94105
Telephone: 415-537-3730
Fax: 415-437-4450
E-mail: frontdesk@chronbooks.com
Web site: www.chroniclebooks.com
Contact: Senior Editor Leslie Jonath

NF, F, J

Having built its book list from regional titles into a world-class publishing operation, Chronicle Books is a market for general nonfiction and fiction, cloth and paperback, including fine arts, gifts, nature, outdoors, nationwide guidebooks, and calendars. Specializing in high-quality, affordable books for adults and children, Chronicle Books is the exclusive U.S. distributor of Princeton Architectural Press and North-South Books. Its "mission is to create and distribute exceptional publishing that is instantly recognizable for its spirit, creativity, and value. This mission also informs our business relationships and endeavors be they with customers, authors, vendors, or colleagues." While Chronicle does publish some fiction, it does not publish romances, science fiction, fantasy, westerns, or other genre fiction. Submissions without agents are acceptable, but consult Chronicle's Web site for complete details on the proper submission package. Founded in 1966.

The Continuum International Publishing Group

370 Lexington Ave., Suite 1700
New York, NY 10017-6503
Telephone: 212-953-5858, 800-561-7704
Fax: 212-953-5944
E-mail: contin@tiac.net
Web site: www.continuumbooks.com
Contact: Vice President and Senior Editor Frank Oveis

NF

This is a serious publisher, especially interested in scholarly and professional books for the trade market. It publishes in the fields of literature and criticism, psychology and social thought, performing arts, and women's studies. In September 2000 the group acquired the higher educational textbook program of Letts, with a sharply focused list on covered management and computer textbooks that complemented the Continuum professional educational program in management, hospitality, and teacher education. With offices in London and New York, Continuum International Publishing Group was established in October 1999. Continuum combines the former academic and religious divisions of Cassell PLC in the U.K. and the Continuum Publishing Company in New York.

The Countryman Press

Division of W. W. Norton & Co., Inc.
Mount Tom Bldg.
Route 12 North
Woodstock, VT 05091
Mailing address: P. O. Box 748
Woodstock, VT 05091-0748
Telephone: 802-457-4826, 800-245-4151
Fax: 802-457-1678
E-mail: countrymanpress@wwnorton.com
Web site: www.countrymanpress.com
Contact: Editor-in-Chief Helen A. Whybrow

NF

Essentially a publisher specializing in books about New England, this publisher will also consider books on skiing, travel, nature, walking, and related outdoor subjects. Its Web site notes that "Vermont has always been a place of adventurous outdoorsmen, ardent conservationists, eloquent writers, and practical but inventive Yankees, and we strive to carry on those values and interests in our books." Its list of books includes guidebooks to hiking, biking, and fly fishing in its respected Backcountry series; books on country living subjects such as pond building and herb gardening; and other books on nature, travel, canoeing, and New England. Founded in 1973.

Cricket Books
Division of Carus Publishing
Imprint of Front Street
332 S. Michigan Ave., Suite 1100
Chicago, IL 60604
Telephone: 312-939-1500
Fax: 312-939-8150
E-mail: mills@caruspub.com
Web site: www.cricketmag.com
Contact: Marketing—Maureen Mills

J

A quality publisher of chapter books and middle-grade novels for children seven to twelve, Cricket Books is an imprint of Front Street Books. This publisher's mission includes a goal of encouraging a lifetime enjoyment of reading and an appreciation for literature. Fantasy, realistic fiction, and humor are the main components of the list. Associated with *Cricket* magazine, which for twenty-five years has published the best juvenile materials in its award-winning magazine. At this time, Cricket Books is interested in chapter books and middle-grade novels for ages seven to twelve. Manuscripts should be double-spaced, hard copy only, pages numbered. Include bio, SASE, and return postcard. Detailed submission requirements available at the Web site. Founded in 1997.

M. Evans & Co. Inc.
216 E. 49 St.
New York, NY 10017
Telephone: 212-688-2810
Fax: 212-486-4544
E-mail: mevans@sprynet.com
Web site: www.mevans.com
Contact: President and Editor-in-Chief George C. de Kay

F, NF

With an editor who is a major figure in the industry, M. Evans & Co., Inc.
is an independent and innovative house that has been publishing thought-
provoking titles for over forty years. A book packager in the 1950s, M. Evans
evolved into a publisher on a wide range of topics. This publisher's eclectic
list includes categories in health, self-help, adult fiction, cookbooks, pop
psychology, history, and true crime. Located in the part of Manhattan
referred to as Turtle Bay, M. Evans remains one of the few independent
New York houses in a sea of conglomerates. Founded in 1963.

Grove/Atlantic Inc.
841 Broadway
New York, NY 10003-4793
Telephone: 212-614-7850, 800-521-0178
Fax: 212-614-7886
E-mail: mentrekin@groveatlantic.com
Contact: President and Publisher Morgan Entrekin

F, NF

General fiction and nonfiction, both in hardcover and paperback. A distinguished publisher, now better than ever under new management since
the mid-1990s. Its list is wide-ranging, from belles lettres and poetry to
cookbooks. It only publishes about 100 books a year and it is very, very
selective. Imprints include Atlantic Monthly Press and Grove Press.
While Grove/Atlantic prefers to work with agented authors, its editors
will try to consider unsolicited manuscripts as time allows. It offers no
specific submission guidelines, except that it publishes literate fiction and

serious nonfiction and usually does not publish genre fiction or self-help/how-to books. Founded in 1952.

The Harvard Common Press
535 Albany Street
Boston, MA 02118
Telephone: 617-423-5803, 888-657-3755
Fax: 617-695-9794
Web site: www.harvardcommonpress.com
Contact: Associate Publisher Dan Rosenbery

NF

This is a good bet for books on parenting and family matters. Small but sincere. Its general nonfiction list also contains some cookbooks, small business guides, and travel guides. Its Web site contains a nicely illustrated catalog of available titles and advertises a specialty in regional cookbooks. Founded in 1976.

Harvard University Press
79 Garden St.
Cambridge, MA 02138-1499
Telephone: 617-495-2600
Fax: 617-495-5898
E-mail: firstname_lastname@harvard.edu
        (e.g., aida_donald@harvard.edu)
Web site: www.hup.harvard.edu
Contact: Editor-in-Chief and Assistant Director Aida D. Donald

NF

General scholarly medical and scientific publishing house with exemplary standards, Harvard University Press can boast of having published many Pulitzer prize–winning books. Also the American publisher of the Loeb Classical Library®, which while currently being revised and updated, totals nearly 500 volumes of Greek and Latin texts, with facing English translations and annual sales over 100,000 volumes. In keeping with its scholarly standards, submissions should be accompanied with a curriculum vitae as well as a cover letter, an outline or table of contents, word count, and an introduction or sample chapter. For more information on submissions, consult its Web page. Founded in 1913, although Harvard University did some printing as far back as the 1600s.

Health Communications, Inc.
3201 SW 15 St.
Deerfield Beach, FL 33442-8190
Telephone: 954-360-0909
Fax: 954-360-0034
Web site: www.hci.online.com
Contact: Editor Christine Belleris

NF, F

Home of the *Chicken Soup for the Soul* books, Health Communications, Inc. publishes trade paperbacks on human relationships, psychology and self-help, personal growth, spirituality and inspiration, audio books, and visionary fiction. Founded in 1976. An imprint of Simcha Press.

Henry Holt and Company, Inc.
Unit of Holtzbrinck Publishing Holdings
115 W. 18 St.
New York, NY 10011
Telephone: 212-886-9200, 212-886-9332
Fax: 212-633-0748
E-mail: publicity@hholt.com
Web site: www.henryholt.com
Contact: Executive Editor David Sobel

NF, F, J

This is a modest-sized publishing house that has grown so that it publishes one of the major mystery writers, Sue Grafton, as well as notable children's authors, computer books, dictionaries, and reference books. Based in New York City, Holt publishes approximately 175 books a year, including hardcover fiction and nonfiction; Owl Books (its trade paperback division); Books for Young Readers; Metropolitan Books; and Times Books. Well managed, well financed, and staffed with talented editors. Founded in 1866.

iPublish.com

1271 Avenue of the Americas
New York, NY 10020
Telephone: 212-522-7200
Fax: 212-522-1048
Web site: www.twbookmark.com/features/ipublish/com
Contact: Editorial Director Claire Zion

F, NF

An online publisher recently launched by Time Warner Books, iPublish.com is designed to open new avenues of access for readers and authors as well as sales and distributions for fiction and nonfiction via the Internet. With its own professional staff, iPublish.com expects to offer both established favorite writers as well as newcomers online publishing. New writers would submit their materials to the *iWrite* segment of iPublish.com, where Time Warner editors and reader-members will review submissions and choose new works to be published in both digital and print formats. As of this writing, iPublish.com is still in development. For updates consult its Web site, where you can register for information about submitting materials once the site is fully operational.

Jewish Lights Publishing

A Division of LongHill Partners, Inc.
P.O. Box 237
Sunset Farm Offices, Rt. 4
Woodstock, Vermont 05091
Telephone: 802-457-4000
Fax: 802-457-4004
Web site: www.jewishlights.com
Contact: Vice president and Editor Sandra Korinchak

NF, J
General trade books for both adults and children on spiritual matters, including theology, philosophy, self-help, and healing, as well as history books. Publishes books of a type that often have not been published elsewhere, which reflect the Jewish wisdom tradition for people of all faiths and backgrounds. Jewish Lights publishes authors who are at the forefront of

spiritual thought and experience. Its books are designed to engage, stimulate, and inspire the readers—and to make a difference in the readers' lives. Founded in 1990.

Kensington Publishing Corp.

850 Third Avenue
New York, NY 10022
Telephone: 212-407-1500
Fax: 212-935-0699
Web site: www.kensingtonbooks.com
Contact: Editorial Director Kate Duffy or
     Consulting Editor Hillary Sares

F, NF

A large mass market paperback publisher that specializes in original romances, fiction, westerns, espionage, general nonfiction, men's adventure, and alternative health. Kensington Publishing Corp., an independent publisher that accounts for about 7 percent of all mass market paperback sales in the United States, has nurtured new authors across the entire spectrum of fiction, romance, and nonfiction categories since its inception in 1975. It focuses on profitable niches and uses aggressive marketing techniques to support its books. Through its Kensington, Zebra, and Pinnacle imprints, the company publishes over 500 new books per year and has a backlist of more than 3,000 titles. Manuscripts are solicited. Detailed writing guidelines are available at its Web site.

Leisure Books

Division of Dorchester Publishing Co., Inc.
276 Fifth Ave., Suite 1008
New York, NY 10001
Telephone: 212-725-8811
Fax: 212-532-1054
Web site: www.dorchesterpub.com
Contact: Editorial Director Alicia Condon

F

This is a mass market publisher that has built its list with original fiction in romance, historical romance, westerns and horror, but with a stated "devotion to romance." Since 1970, Leisure and Dorchester have promoted hundreds of first-time authors. Actively seeking new writers for its Western series. Manuscripts are solicited. Very specific instructions on just what type of fiction it is currently seeking, along with writers' guidelines, available at its Web site.

Menasha Ridge Press
700 S. 28 St., Suite 206
Birmingham, AL 35233
Telephone: 205-322-0439, 800-247-9437
Fax: 205-326-1012
E-mail: info@menasharidge.com
Web site: www.menasharidge.com
Contact: President and Publisher Robert W. Sehlinger

NF

A publisher of nonfiction books, Menasha Ridge Press is a leading publisher of outdoor recreation, travel, and reference books. Its authors are chosen from the best known and most capable in their fields. Founded in 1982.

Newmarket Press
Division of Newmarket Publishing & Communications Co.
18 E. 48 St.
New York, NY 100177
Telephone: 212-832-3575, 800-669-3903
Fax: 212-832-3629
E-mail: mailbox@newmarketpress.com
Web site: www.newmarketpress.com
Contact: President and Publisher Esther Margolis

F, NF

This publisher, known for its movie tie-ins, also publishes highly visible books in consumer reference, self-help, and investment. Hardback, trade paperbacks, fiction, and general nonfiction are available from Newmarket Press. Founded in 1981.

W. W. Norton & Company Trade Department

Division of W. W. Norton & Company Inc.
500 Fifth Ave.
New York, NY 10110-0017
Telephone: 212-354-5500
Fax: 212-869-0856
Web site: www.wwnorton.com
Contact: Editor Edwin Barber

F, NF

A division of W. W. Norton & Company, the oldest and largest publishing house owned wholly by its employees, the Trade Department expands W. W. Norton beyond its college books and Norton Anthology offerings into the popular book market. Among its current titles, W. W. Norton boasts that it publishes Bill Clinton's favorite mystery writer. Founded in 1923.

The Overlook Press

Subsidiary of Peter Mayer Publishers, Inc.
386 W. Broadway
New York, NY 10012
Telephone: 212-965-8400
Fax: 212-965-9834
Web site: www.overlook.com
Contact: CEO and President Peter Mayer

F, NF

Peter Mayer, the former chief executive of Penguin Books, is now actively involved in this company founded by his father. The Overlook Press publishes fiction, general nonfiction, theatre, biography, art, architecture, history, design, film, popular culture, hardcover reprints, and trade paperbacks. This company's list will grow in size and diversity. Overlook prefers to work with agented authors, but will accept traditional (not e-mail) query letters from unagented authors. Founded in 1971, it publishes about seventy-five titles annually.

Pineapple Press, Inc.
P.O. Box 3899
Sarasota, FL 34230
Telephone: 941-359-0886
Fax: 941-351-9988
E-mail: info@pineapplepress.com
Web site: www.Pineapplepress.com
Contact: Executive Editor June Cussen

NF, F

If you have a book about Florida, the Southwest, or nature, this is indeed a best bet. A publisher of primarily nonfiction books related to Florida, Pineapple Press does now publish a few, select literary novels and some non-Florida nature books. It also now publishes a growing list of books not specifically related to Florida, including fundraising for nonprofits, light-houses and lighthouse keepers, and ghosts. However, as its Web site notes, its primary focus is on books about Florida. It does not publish children's books with the possible exception of those with Florida topics for Florida schools. It does not publish genre fiction (mysteries, romances, science fiction, action/adventure, westerns) unless they are strongly Florida related. Founded in 1982, it does accept queries from nonagented writers. Its submission requirements are detailed at its Web site. In general, they require a query letter, a brief synopsis, first three chapters, and a SASE.

Pleasant Company Publications
Subsidiary of Pleasant Company
8400 Fairway Place
Middleton, WI 53562
Telephone: 608-836-4848
Fax: 608-836-1999
Web site: www.americangirl.com
Contact: Editorial Director Judy Woodburn

J

A publisher that specializes in books for girls in the 8–13 age range, Pleasant Company publishes both quality and positive-minded fiction and non-fiction of interest to girls in that age bracket. The American Girls

Collection® is Pleasant Company's best-known historical fiction imprint. The books in this collection, which tell the stories of American girls who lived long ago, are written and produced by Pleasant Company's own team of authors and editors. However, Pleasant Company does accept manuscripts and manuscript queries in other areas for quality fiction and nonfiction. Its Web site notes the company's interest in developing authors for History Mysteries®, a series for girls ages 10–12 (a fifth-grade reading level). Each book in the series stands alone, with its own characters, time period, and geographical setting. While authors may submit a complete manuscript for History Mysteries® submissions, Pleasant Company prefers to see a detailed proposal that includes a plot outline, a sample chapter, a description of the historical setting, and a list or samples of previous publications. History Mysteries® submissions should conform to the specific guidelines available at its Web site. Pleasant Company also seeks manuscripts for AG Fiction™, its new contemporary middle-grade fiction imprint. These novels capture the spirit and voices of contemporary American girls and feature an 11-to-13-year-old protagonist who demonstrates the hopes, thoughts, and emotions of that age. Again, detailed submission guidelines for this are available at its Web site.

Regnery Publisher, Inc.

Subsidiary of Eagle Publishing
One Massachusetts Ave. NW
Washington, DC 20001
Telephone: 202-216-0600
Fax: 202-216-0612
Web site: www.regnery.com
Contact: Publisher and President Alfred S. Regnery

NF

A publisher of choice for authors of books that appeal to a politically conservative reading audience. Regnery Publisher prints nonfiction trade books, paperbacks, and college paperbound classics. Founded in 1947.

Running Press Book Publishers

125 S. 22 St.
Philadelphia, PA 19103-4399
Telephone: 215-567-5080
Fax: 215-568-2919
Web site: www.runningpress.com
Contact: Publisher Stuart Teacher

NF, J

Stylishly designed books for house and home, art, science, and children.
Running Press specializes in publishing illustrated nonfiction for adults
and children. It very rarely publishes any new fiction or poetry and is not
seeking submissions in those categories at this time. Running Press does
publish hardcover and paperback trade books on art, crafts, how-to, general nonfiction, children's books, promotional books, stationery, notebooks,
journals, and Miniature Editions™. Running Press books cover a wide
range of subjects, from photo-essays on relationships to explorations of the
world, to cookbooks from some of America's finest restaurants, and kits
and discovery books for children. Specific submission guidelines at its Web
site suggest interested writers submit a query letter with a brief outline or
table of contents. Founded in 1972.

Shambhala Publications, Inc.

Horticultural Hall
300 Massachusetts Ave.
Boston, MA 02115
Mailing address: P.O. Box 308
Boston, MA 02117
Telephone: 617-424-0030
Fax: 617-236-1563
E-mail: editors@shambhala.com
Web site: www.shambhala.com
Contact: President and Executive Editor Peter Turner

NF

Shambhala publishes trade books with emphasis on art, literature, compar-
ative religion, philosophy, science, psychology, and spiritual matters.

Founded in California during the 1960s counterculture era, Shambhala still favors metaphysical books. Named for Shambhala, a legendary Central Asian kingdom that symbolizes an enlightened way of life harmonizing the inner and outer worlds. Accepts queries from writers without agents, but advises that authors should follow the guidelines at its Web site and that it publishes very little contemporary fiction, poetry, art, or children's books. Founded in 1969.

Silhouette Books

300 E. 42 St., 6th Floor
New York, NY 10017
Telephone: 212-682-6080
Fax: 212-682-4539
Web sites: www.romance.net, www.eharlequin.com
Contact: Editorial Director Tara Gavin

F

Perhaps best known for its romance novels, Silhouette Books publishes adult contemporary, historical romance novels, and women's fiction. It has special categories of romance novels from "Desire" to "Intimate Moments" to "Romance" with its more traditional values. Its Web site has an intriguing "Learn to Write" section, with links to similar sites. Detailed submission guidelines are available at www.eharlequin.com. Multiple submissions are not acceptable. A literary agent is not required in order to submit. Query first, following the details for submissions available on the Web. Founded in 1979.

Stackpole Books

5067 Ritter Road
Mechanicsburg, PA 17055
Telephone: 717-796-0411
Fax: 717-796-0412
Web site: www.stackpolebooks.com
Contact: Vice President and Editorial Director Judith Schnell

NF

A publisher of quality hardcovers and paperbacks on the outdoors, fishing, nature, sports, crafts and hobbies, carving, gardening, photography, woodworking, military, reference, history, and Pennsylvania. Its Web site contains specific e-mail addresses by category for authors to query regarding the specific needs and submission requirements. Founded in 1933 as a small, family-owned publishing house.

Storey Books
Division of Storey Communications, Inc.
105 Schoolhouse Road
Pownal, VT 05261
Telephone: 802-823-5200
Fax: 802-823-5819
E-mail: info@storey.com
Web site: www.storey.com
Contact: President, CEO, and Publisher Pamela Art

NF, J

A Vermont-based publishing company, Storey now publishes under the imprints Storey Books and Storey's Books for Country Living. Storey specializes in how-to books for country living, including gardening, natural health and beauty, herbs, cooking and food preservation, building, crafts, equestrian, animals, and home brewing, with some children's nonfiction. Its gardening books are consistent best-sellers. Founded in 1983.

Time Warner Trade Publishing
Division of AOL Time Warner Co.
Subsidiary of iPublish.com
1271 Avenue of the Americas
New York, NY 10020
Telephone: 212-522-7200
Fax: 212-522-7991
Web site: www.twbookmark.com
Contact: President Maureen Mahon Egen

F, NF

Time Warner publishes hardback, trade paperbacks, mass market fiction, and nonfiction. Currently only the Warner Romance imprint is accepting manuscript queries from nonagented writers. Since Warner Romance Publishing's historical and contemporary romances are not written to any formula, it does not have a tip sheet, but looks for well-plotted, sensual love stories between likable characters in a realistic and interesting setting. Its romance books are usually between 90,000 and 110,000 words. Submission guidelines for its romance line are available at the Web site.

Walker & Co.
Division of Walker Publishing Co., Inc.
435 Hudson St.
New York, NY 10014
Telephone: 212-727-8300
Fax: 212-727-0984
Web site: www.walkerbooks.com
Contact: President and Publisher George L. Gibson

F, NF, J

Trade publisher in the areas of health, sports, history, careers, self-help, parenting, personal investment, mysteries, and children's books. Walker is an independent, 40-year-old, family-owned publisher founded in 1959. From the start, Walker has been diverse, reflecting its original owners' varied tastes, many of which continue to define its list today. History in its many guises has always been an active part of its list, and it has crime mystery and children's divisions as well. Will accept queries from unagented writers with a complete synopsis, SASE, and the first chapter. Prefers nontraditional crime mysteries. Will e-mail submission requirements in response to brief e-mail query about submissions.

Workman Publishing Company Inc.
708 Broadway
New York, NY 10003-9555
Telephone: 212-254-5900
Fax: 212-254-8098
E-mail: mged@workman.com
Web site: www.workmanweb.com
Contact: Editor-in-Chief Sally Kovalchick

NF

Workman publishes general nonfiction, calendars, and a large collection of gardening books. For insight of specifically what type of books it prints, visit the online catalog at its Web site. Will accept unsolicited manuscripts. They have no specific guidelines. Founded in 1967, it published forty-five titles in 1999.

Xlibris
A strategic partner of Random House Ventures
Telephone: 888-795-4274
Web site: www.xlibris.com

Xlibris, a strategic partner of Random House Ventures, offers an array of online publishing services with fees ranging from modest to more than a thousand dollars.

Aside from relatively low costs to the author and a nonjudgmental acceptance policy, Xlibris offers a "publish on demand" option that allows writers access to publishing power through a digital manufacturing process that does not involve the high costs and risks of traditional publishing.

Xlibris also offers authors the comfort of acceptance. Any author can submit his or her manuscript following submission instructions available from Xlibris's Web site, www.xlibris.com. The professional staff of Xlibris then works with the author to design the interior and cover of the book, which when completed is available on demand to the readers. Xlibris pays royalties ranging from 10 to 50 percent, and allows the authors to keep all rights to the manuscript, as well as registers the resulting product with such well known online booksellers as amazon.com, BarnesandNoble.com and

Borders.com. For extra fees, Xlibris can also provide Library of Congress card catalog numbers, U.S. copyright registration, and a CD-ROM archive. A purely publishing service, Xlibris does not make any judgments about the quality of the manuscript and does not edit documents, though a copy-editing service is available for an additional fee.

While the basic, "core" service was initially available to writers for free, Xlibris announced in early 2001 that it would now be charging a $200 fee for the formerly free service, as well as raising the fees for the more premier services that had always been fee based. The differences in services (and fees) relate to such matters as whether an author's photograph will be included and how unique a cover will be.

Authors considering this option should check with the Web site, which provides detailed information on services, fees, and submission steps. However, the basic requirements are that the materials be in English, no less than 30,000 words, and no more than 180,000 words. Submissions will be accepted on disk, by e-mail, or from the Web, and for an additional fee even paper copies are accepted.

Drawbacks to publishing with Xlibris include the lack of marketing and editorial assistance, valuable services usually provided by traditional publishing companies, as well as a potential vanity press stigma.

APPENDIX D

Manuscript Submission Record

Because you will probably be submitting your manuscript to more than one publisher, you should maintain a record of when and to whom you submitted the manuscript and the responses you receive. All agents do this.

A submission form you can use is shown on page 233.

Manuscript Submission Record

Sent to: _____
                    (PUBLISHER)

_____
            (ADDRESS)   (ZIP CODE)

Name of editor:_____ Passed on to: _____

Telephone number:_____ Fax number: _____

E-mail:_____

Date sent:_____ Follow-up date: _____

Response: _____

Additional information: _____

_____

_____

_____

Sent to: _____
                    (PUBLISHER)

_____
            (ADDRESS)   (ZIP CODE)

Name of editor:_____ Passed on to:_____

Telephone number:_____ Fax number: _____

E-mail:_____

Date sent:_____ Follow-up date: _____

Response: _____

Additional information: _____

_____

_____

_____

About the Author

Martin Levin has spent more than half a century in the publishing business, as a publisher, agent, teacher, and publishing lawyer. He joined Grosset & Dunlap in 1950 as the Assistant to the Assistant Sales Manager of their subsidiary Wonder Books. This is about as far down the ladder as one can get. Moving up through the company, he became Senior Vice President of the parent company and a member of the Board of Directors in 1960. In his sixteen years at Grosset, he was involved in every aspect of publishing and participated in the explosive growth of the juvenile, adult fiction, and non-fiction lists, both in hardcover and paperback.

In 1966, the Times Mirror Company invited him to become President of their Book Group. Times Mirror at that time was primarily a newspaper publisher, and they were just building their book publishing business. Mr. Levin oversaw such distinguished trade book companies as New American Library, Harry N. Abrams, and World Publishing Company and several leading professional book publishing companies owned by Times Mirror. In his seventeen years at Times Mirror, Mr. Levin was deeply involved in the publication of the first paperback books by Stephen King, Robin Cook, Erica Jong, and scores of others. During this period, he was also elected Chairman of the American Association of Publishers, was on the first publishers' mission to China after the Cultural Revolution, and was a pioneer in developing publishing relations with the Soviet Union.

At sixty-one years of age, Mr. Levin decided it was time to achieve his lifelong dream of becoming a lawyer. While still in charge of the Times Mirror Book Group, he enrolled in New York Law School and studied at night for four years. When he reached age sixty-five in June 1983, he graduated from law school. He retired from his position at Times Mirror in January 1984. He took the bar examination in February 1984, passed, and was admitted to practice in June 1984.

In January 1985, Mr. Levin joined the distinguished intellectual property firm of Cowan, Liebowitz & Latman in New York. For the last seventeen years, he has counseled and represented authors as well as negotiated their contracts. He has lectured at the Stanford University Professional Publishing Course each year and has taught Publishing Law as an Adjunct Professor for the last fourteen years at New York Law School. His "Eight-Step Program" grew out of his publishing and legal experiences. Mr. Levin has also been very actively involved in representing publishers in the sale of their businesses. In 1999, the Association of American Publishers awarded Mr. Levin the Curtis Benjamin Award for lifetime achievement in publishing.

The Levin family has a history of involvement in publishing, entertainment, and education. Marcia Levin, his wife, is a writer of children's books, with over twenty books to her credit. Jeremy Leven (slight change in the spelling) is an author, screenwriter, and director. His films include *Creator, Don Juan de Marco,* and *Bagger Vance.* He is also the author of two best-selling novels. Dr. Wendy Levin Newby created and directed a learning disabilities clinic in Raleigh and is now an Assistant Dean at Emory University in Atlanta. Hugh Lauter Levin has been a publisher for over twenty-five years. He was a Vice President of the distinguished art book publisher Harry N. Abrams for ten years. In 1973 he founded his own art book publishing house, Hugh Lauter Levin Associates, which is now considered to be one of the most creative and successful independent art book publishers in the world.

INDEX